An Introduction to British Civil Registration

Tom Wood

Published by
The Federation of Family History Societies (Publications) Ltd
Units 15-16 Chesham Ind. Est., Oram Street, Bury, Lancs BL9 6EN

First Published 1994
Second Edition 2000

ISBN 1 86006 116 8

Printed and bound by The Alden Group, Oxford and Northampton

Contents

Introduction

Three main events

Most family historians will find researching their immediate ancestors involves using the 'Statutory Records of Civil Registration' of births, deaths and marriages. We should all know that by law nowadays when babies are born their births have to be locally registered and when people die their deaths have to be locally registered too, mainly for statistical purposes. Many of us, also, may even have chosen to marry in a local register office, and even if we married in a church or chapel our personal details on that day were similarly recorded in an official marriage register. As we go through life we sometimes need authentic copies, or certificates, of these events to prove who we are, how old we are or when we married and to whom, and when we die we cannot be buried or cremated without having a death certificate. So the three main events in people's lives, of birth, death and marriage, are now officially recorded by state authorities and as family historians we are able to avail ourselves of the earlier records of civil registration to trace our ancestors. At the worst today everyone should eventually end up with at least birth and death registrations and certificates. Most of us will have a marriage certificate, and some people will have more than one of these!

So why do family historians find these records so useful? Well most of us will know when our parents' birthdays were and when they married, but when it comes to knowing when our grandparents' birthdays were things may not be so clear. And when it comes to knowing when our grandparents married then many of us are often completely stumped. If we go back to earlier generations of our ancestors, often in the 19th century, then our knowledge of the three main events in their lives may be almost nothing. Indeed most family historians will need to consult the records of civil registration at quite an early stage to confirm or establish when their ancestors were born, died, or married. Birth certificates tell us where and when people were born and the names of both parents, including the mother's maiden surname, and with this information we can begin a search for the parents' marriage. Marriage certificates should tell us where and when marriages took place, the ages of the couple (not always accurate) and who their respective fathers were. Armed with this information we can seek the birth registrations of the bride and groom. Death certificates contain more limited genealogical information, but we should never disregard them as ages from them can be used to assist searches for births and may point the way to other helpful records like wills or other probate records. Scottish certificates are the most informative of all in the British Isles.

In England and Wales civil registration of births, deaths and marriages began 1 July 1837, in Scotland 1 January 1855 and in Ireland 1 January 1864 (with non-Catholic marriages from 1845). There were also independent systems of civil registration on the Isle of Man from 1858, and on the Channel Islands from the 1840s. The system used by earlier generations of your family depends where your ancestors lived. It is important from an early stage to ascertain this as the various British systems require different approaches. Each British system has various local and national indexes and different methods of accessing the indexes. Sometimes various events can be confirmed merely by finding events in the indexes, but most family historians will usually find it necessary also to obtain a number of copy certificates. Copies of certificates of registrations have to be purchased for fees from the various civil registration authorities.

Before searching for events in the various systems it can sometimes be worthwhile checking on the International Genealogical Index (IGI) in case births and marriages are already recorded, in abbreviated format, during the early periods of civil registration in the nineteenth century. The IGI is now generally available either on microfiche or on CD-ROM in many Family History Centres (small genealogical research units attached to many Mormon churches, where anyone can undertake genealogical research by appointment; see Appendix II), at county record offices and larger reference libraries, etc. The IGI is also on the Internet at: www.familysearch.org/

A limited number of abbreviated civil registration entries of births and marriages are also listed in the 'Vital Records Index – British Isles' (BIVRI) available for sale on CD-ROM from the Church of Jesus Christ of Latter-day Saints, The Distribution Centre, 399 Garretts Green Lane, Birmingham B33 0UH (Tel: 0121-785-2200). It should also be available to search (not for sale) at LDS Church Family History Centres. It may be worth checking as a long-shot.

Search fees and certificate costs

Because the different fees charged for certificates and searches are subject to change without warning, those effective on publication have not been included in the text. However a schedule of charges operative in the Summer of 2000 is included at the back of this volume to provide newcomers with at least an idea of the different costings. Unfortunately rescheduling of certificate and search costs is usually upwards! Current costs of certificates can be obtained by telephoning the main national offices or from their websites.

CAUTION.

CONVICTIONS FOR GIVING FALSE INFORMATION TO A REGISTRAR RESPECTING A DEATH.

On 14th May, 1877, **Gilbert L—** was **charged** before the Magistrates at Plymouth **with having**, on 5th April last, offended against the Provisions of the 40th Section of the Births and Deaths Registration Act, 1874, **by giving to the Registrar** of the St. Andrew's Sub-District **False Information respecting the Death of Sarah Jane G—**; he having **falsely stated that the Name** of the deceased **was Sarah Jane L—**, and that she **was his Wife.**

The Defendant was summarily convicted, and was sentenced to pay a **Fine of Five Pounds** or to undergo **One Month's Imprisonment.**

On the 31st August, 1877, **George B—** appeared before the Magistrates at Leeds to **answer the charge of having** on 13th inst., **made a False Statement to the Registrar** of the West Sub-District of Leeds, **respecting the Death of a Child**; thereby offending against the Provisions of the 40th Section of the Births and Deaths Registration Act, 1874.

The Defendant was Summarily Convicted and was Fined Five Pounds.

The 40th Section of the Births and Deaths Registration Act, 1874, enacts as follows :—

Any person who commits any of the following Offences ; that is to say—

(1.) Wilfully makes any False Answer to any question put to him by a Registrar relating to the particulars required to be registered concerning any Birth or Death, or wilfully gives to a Registrar any False Information concerning any Birth or Death, or the Cause of any Death; or,

(2.) Wilfully makes any False Certificate or Declaration under or for the purposes of this Act, or forges or falsifies any such Certificate or Declaration, or any Order under this Act, or, knowing any such Certificate, Declaration, or Order to be false or forged, uses the same as true, or gives or sends the same as true to any person; or,

(3.) Wilfully makes, gives, or uses any False Statement or Representation as to a Child born alive having been Still-born, or as to the body of a Deceased Person or a Still-born Child in any coffin, or falsely pretends that any Child born alive was Still-born ; or,

(4.) Makes any False Statement with intent to have the same entered in any Register of Births or Deaths ;

shall for each Offence be liable on Summary Conviction to a Penalty not exceeding Ten Pounds, and on Conviction on Indictment to Fine or to Imprisonment with or without Hard Labour for a Term not exceeding Two Years, or to Penal Servitude for a Term not exceeding Seven Years.

Caution No. 3 A.   P & T 600 1—70

There have always been penalties for perjury.

SECTION 1

England and Wales

The system of civil registration in England and Wales is the oldest in Great Britain and Ireland and began on 1 July 1837, in the same year as Queen Victoria ascended the throne. All family historians with ancestors in England and Wales will surely lament the fact that an attempt to introduce 'comprehensive and compulsory' registration of births and deaths in 1753 was defeated by the House of Lords. Largely, it has to be said, because the Bill also sought to introduce proposals for carrying out a census of the population. Although censuses were later introduced in 1801, it was not until the *Births and Deaths Registration Act* and *The Marriage Act*, both of 1836, were passed that the Office of the Registrar General (of England and Wales) was established in London and the system of statutory recording of births, deaths and marriages for statistical purposes was set up.

Registrations and Registration Districts
The countries were divided up into administrative areas known as 'Registration Districts', each in the charge of a 'Superintendent Registrar'. These registration districts were based on the existing 'Poor Law Unions', or groups of parishes which usually supported a central communal workhouse where those unfortunates in want were then housed and fed. Many of the original registration districts have been absorbed into others or their original area of coverage modified and quite a number have been abolished or incorporated into newer ones. Within each registration district were sub-districts where the responsibility for recording births and deaths initially lay with a local registrar appointed to that sub-district. Three maps showing the locations of the different registration districts (and census districts) of England and Wales for 1837–1851, 1852-1946 and 1946-1965 have been produced by and may be bought from The Institute of Heraldic and Genealogical Studies, 80–82 Northgate, Canterbury, Kent CT1 1BA. Send a stamped self-addressed envelope for prices (or check its website at: www.ihgs.ac.uk).

An Internet website (www.fhsc.org.uk/genuki/reg) identifies registration districts in England and Wales from 1837 to 1930, by county and then lists the parishes in each. A useful 'Index of Places in England and Wales, 1837–1930' is also available on the Internet and identifies the registration district for any given place. It can be found at:
www.genuki.org.uk/big/eng/civreg/places/

From 1837 to 1874, when the *Births and Deaths Registration Act* transferred the obligation to register births and deaths to the persons concerned, it was up to local registrars to travel around their sub-districts and record these events, within 42 days for births and usually within 5 days for deaths. Informants could only be prosecuted if they refused to supply the registrar with the details of a birth or death. They were bound by law to answer the registrar's questions, but were not at that time legally obliged to report a birth or death. In some parts of England and Wales it is estimated that up to 15 per cent of births went unregistered until 1875 when the above Act transferred the onus for registration to the parents or immediate family. This can be a reason why some births, and occasionally deaths, cannot be found in the early years of civil registration. Don't forget there was quite widespread illiteracy amongst many working class families in early Victorian times, so people could not always read and understand public notices. Some parents thought they could continue to have their children baptised in a church or chapel as an alternative to birth registration. Others feared their children would be forced to be vaccinated against smallpox if their births were registered. Quite stiff penalty payments could be enforced for late registrations which sometimes caused parents to conceal the arrival of their children from the registrar, or to 'forward date' births by several weeks if registering a child after the customary six weeks allowed for registration had elapsed.

The 1874 Act also tightened up the registration of illegitimate births. Until 1874 the mother of an illegitimate child could name whoever she chose as the father of her child and the registrar was bound to accept it. From 1875 the father could only be named on the birth registration of an illegitimate child if he accompanied the mother to register the child and gave information jointly with her. In connection with illegitimate offspring the *Legitimacy Act of 1926* made provision for children born out of wedlock to be legitimated by re-registration on the subsequent marriage of their parents, providing neither parent was already married to a third party when the child was born. Also in 1926 an Act authorised the Registrar General to maintain an 'Adopted Children Register' and from 1927, for the first time, all still-births had to be notified and registered.

The Births and Deaths Registration Act of 1874 also made it compulsory for all death registrations to be supported by a medical certificate specifying the causes of death and signed by a qualified medical practitioner who attended the dead person. Before the 1874 Act the causes of death could be guesswork by the informant.

Marriage registrations were rather more complicated. Arrangements for the introduction of civil marriage ceremonies in local register offices from mid-1837 did not affect the arrangement whereby the Established Church (Church of England and Church in Wales) carried on with their religious marriage ceremonies, although a more comprehensive official form of marriage register was introduced on 1 July 1837 and all marriages in the Established Church had to be notified quarterly to the Registrar General. Nor did the new legislation affect marriages of Jews or Quakers. Since 1754 these two dissenting religious groups had been granted special concessions to enable them to carry out their own marriages and they were the only two denominations legally allowed to conduct their own ceremonies. When civil registration began they were allowed to continue these ceremonies, but they also had to conform to the new statutory regulations and supply full details of their marriages every quarter to the Registrar General.

All other religious denominations, if they wished, could apply for their churches or chapels to be registered for marriages from mid-1837 and, until the *Marriage Act of 1898* (effective 1899), ceremonies could only take place in them in the presence of a local registrar who recorded the marriage in a marriage register which belonged to the local register office. *The Marriage Act of 1898* allowed nonconformist congregations from 1899 to appoint 'authorised persons' to solemnise their own marriages in their own registered churches or chapels and have their own marriage registers and so dispense with the attendance of local register office officials and their registers. The problems of arranging for local register office officials to attend at most nonconformist marriages before 1899 is one of the reasons why many nonconformist couples chose to marry either in the Church of England or have a civil ceremony at the local register office.

Civil marriage ceremonies in register offices in the 19th century were the cheapest way of marrying, but initially were rather unpopular. In more recent times, following *The Marriage Act of 1994*, civil marriage ceremonies, in the presence of a registrar, have been extended to a range of different secular locations, subject to approval as per the terms of the Act. Such marriages are registered in the same way as all other ceremonies. Researchers are also reminded that in the recent past it has become increasingly fashionable for couples to marry in so-called 'romantic places' overseas. Such overseas marriages have no documentation in England or Wales.

The Age of Marriage Act of 1929 made the minimum age for marriage with parental consent 16 years (hitherto it had been 12 for girls and 14 for boys, though marriages at such tender years rarely took place) and further legislation in the 20th century lifted some of the restrictions on people who were not previously permitted to marry each other through some family relationship. Most notable of these were the *Deceased Wife's Sister's Marriage Act of 1907* (allowing men to marry their deceased wife's sister, although the clergy retained a right to refuse such marriages) and the *Deceased Brother's Widow's Marriage Act of 1921* (allowing marriage between a man and his deceased brother's widow). In 1969 the age of majority was reduced from 21 to 18 years and it then became the new age for marriage without parental consent.

LOCAL AND NATIONAL INDEXES

Under the terms for the establishment of civil registration, in England and Wales in 1837, every quarter every superintendent registrar in each registration district had to supply the Registrar General with full details of all births and deaths registrations recorded in their registration district. They also had to supply full quarterly details of civil marriages conducted in their local register offices and up to 1899 of nonconformist marriages recorded and registered in their register office marriage registers. These events concerning births, deaths and civil marriages were also separately indexed by the staff in local register offices (marriages under the surnames of both the bride and the groom).

It was also the responsibility of all incumbents conducting marriages in the Established Church, together with Quaker registering officers and

Jewish rabbis, to submit a quarterly return, showing full details of all marriage entries from their registers. From 1899 'authorised persons' from other registered nonconformist churches or chapels were also required to make a similar quarterly return of their marriages. These quarterly marriage returns were submitted to local superintendent registrars, who passed them onto the Registrar General with their own quarterly returns of births, deaths and civil marriages. Until fairly recent times it was not usual for superintendent registrars to index these quarterly marriage details from churches and chapels as they passed through their hands on their way to the Registrar General in London.

Once with the Registrar General the full particulars of the quarterly returns were copied into national registers of births, deaths and marriages. Next they were nationally indexed (marriages under the names of both the bride and groom) in quarters, with separate alphabetical indexes for births, deaths and marriages. These quarterly indexes list events by surname, then Christian name(s) followed by the name of the registration district where the event was registered, and finally references (volume and page number) to locate that particular entry in the copy registers held by the Registrar General. It has to be emphasised here that as a result of the copied information being passed on, that the registers held by the Registrar General are copies of copies of the original entries in the respective local registers, and from time to time errors and sometimes omissions did occur through poor handwriting or misreading. This can account for omissions or mis-indexing of events in these national indexes.

The fact that both the church and the civil authorities were permitted to preside over marriage ceremonies from 1837 complicates the recording and indexing arrangements at local register office level. The personal details recorded at marriage ceremonies in the various churches or chapels, authorised to keep their own marriage registers, were always entered in two separate identical marriage registers. Both registers were kept in the parish in the case of the Established Churches, or with the congregation in the case of other denominations as outlined above. Only when a marriage register was completely full with marriage registrations, or when a church or chapel closed, was one copy of the marriage register deposited with the local superintendent registrar, and only then could it be locally indexed under the name of the church or chapel. Thus family historians hoping to locate marriages through local register offices, in addition to the date, must know the name of the church or building where the event took place. Because of these complications in register offices, marriages are most easily located in the national quarterly indexes of the Registrar General if they took place at all. Nowadays the second copy of a marriage register from churches or chapels (when full or no longer used), is frequently deposited with other church or chapel registers in the appropriate Diocesan, or County Record, Office.

To sum up, there are always two sets of indexes to births and deaths since 1837, one held in the register office where the event was first recorded, and a second national index covering all events throughout England and Wales held by the Registrar General. There are also national indexes to all marriages, irrespective of religious or civil ceremonies, for the whole of England and Wales since 1837 which are also held by the Registrar General. Finally there are indexes to some marriages, including all civil ceremonies, in local register offices, but if the marriage took place in a church or chapel you will usually only be able to secure a copy certificate if the exact details are known and the appropriate marriage register has been deposited (as above) with the local superintendent registrar. Unfortunately few register offices have produced unified marriage indexes to all the marriages recorded in deposited registers from churches or chapels within their registration districts.

ACCESS TO THE INDEXES IN ENGLAND AND WALES

The public has a right of access to the indexes in the custody of both the Registrar General and those held in local register offices, but under different circumstances. However the public has no right of access to the actual registers. If you require details from a registration, then you have to purchase a copy certificate.

The Family Records Centre (FRC)

The Family Records Centre, 1 Myddelton Street, London EC1R 1UW (Tel: 020-8392-5300, and 020-7233-9233 for certificate enquiries ordered in London) became the main London repository for the national collections of index volumes to the registers of civil registration in England and Wales when St Catherine's House closed in spring 1997. The premises are shared between the Office for National Statistics, on the ground floor, and the

Public Record Office (Central London Reading Room) on the first floor which mainly houses filmed copies of English and Welsh census returns over 100 years old. Myddelton Street is located just off Rosebery Avenue near Finsbury Town Hall. The nearest underground station is Angel (Northern Line) at Islington and researchers on foot should turn left when leaving the station into St John Street and walk along until turning right into Rosebery Avenue (the route is signposted). Rosebery Avenue is on the 38, 19 and 341 London bus routes which stop nearby. In addition service 63 runs up and down Farringdon Road a few hundred yards away. It is also within slightly further walking distance from Farringdon underground station (Hammersmith and City, Circle and Metropolitan underground lines, plus Thameslink). The FRC is also very close to London Metropolitan Archives, at 40 Northampton Road, London EC1R 0HP, for researchers with interests in parish records, etc, from the Greater London area.

Access to the Family Records Centre is free to all ages and without individual appointments. However the centre would appreciate advance warning of large group visits to avoid overcrowding (Tel: 020-7533-6438). It is open on normal weekdays as follows: Mondays, Wednesday and Fridays 9.00am to 5.00pm, Tuesdays 10.00am to 7.00pm, Thursdays 9.00am to 7.00pm and Saturdays 9.30am to 5.00pm. Family historians are advised not to take along disinterested companions although there are good rest areas with seating facilities. The busiest times are on Tuesdays, Thursdays and Saturdays, especially during school holidays, and the 'hectic hours' from 11.30am to 2.30 pm daily. You are advised to wear comfortable working clothes as the indexes can be bulky to use. Comfortable footwear is recommended too, as you must stand to find events in the indexes. Anyone who cannot manage the heavy indexes can look at them on microfiche (which are very widely available elsewhere; see Appendix I), but the numbers of microfiche readers are limited and this service should be booked in advance (Tel: 020-7533-6438). Cumbersome articles like large handbags, brief cases, umbrellas and back packs can be deposited in self-operated luggage lockers (using refundable coins) whilst coats can be left in lockable coat racks, both located in the basement cloakroom. Personal items containing valuables, particularly ladies' handbags, should never be left unattended in the searchrooms. The seasoned researcher at the FRC uses a fairly small notebook and a pencil (fountain pens or biros may be needed to complete application sheets for certificates, but must not be used when searching in the indexes) and makes notes of all searches including the negative ones. There is a spacious refreshment area in the basement with basic vending machines or visitors may also bring their own consumables. Disabled facilities are very good (very limited nearby disabled parking must be pre-booked on 020-7533-6436) and good toilet facilities are available on all floors. There is also a baby changing room in the basement. Smoking is totally banned throughout the FRC and mobile phones should be switched off during visits. For visitors needing to use a telephone the centre has a number of pay-phones, including a BT Multiphone which can be used to despatch e-mails, etc. The use of self-powered electronic recording equipment is permitted.

Searching in the indexes

Researchers should be prepared to check several different surname spellings, if an event cannot be located under its expected spelling (see also *Problems with Names*, below, under 'Failed Searches and Civil Registration Problems'). It is also sometimes worthwhile bearing in mind that shortened versions of Christian names were sometimes used, particularly on marriage. So that under a common surname listing, Polly will be some way from Mary, Ted some way from Edward, Beckie some way from Rebecca, and Kit some way from Christopher, etc, in the indexes.

There are separate sections at the FRC for the national indexes to births, marriages and deaths. They relate to events by quarter from 1837 to 1983 inclusive (i.e. events registered each year in the 3 monthly periods ending March, June, September and December). Therefore to search a full year involves searching in four separate indexes and some events, especially births, for which a period of six weeks is allowed for registration, may have been registered in the quarter after the one in which they took place. This does not apply to marriage registrations that should always be registered in the quarter in which they took place. Events registered since 1984 are recorded in an annual index for each event. Researchers are not allocated individual desk space and the quarterly indexes can be rather heavy and bulky. The ideal situation is to work from a desk space in front of the shelving where the indexes of interest are stored. Your right to a particular desk space on the sloping desks where the indexes should be searched has to be closely guarded at busy times. If you have to keep leaving your desk space to replace or obtain indexes from distant shelves you may easily find your space invaded by other researchers in your absence.

Free information from the GRO indexes

Certain useful 'free' information appears in the national indexes that can be very helpful in positively identifying events for family historians. Since the September quarter of 1911 the mother's maiden surname appears in the births indexes, which enables researchers to construct family units of brothers and sisters without buying actual certificates and can also be useful in locating marriages of the parents. A mother's maiden surname that is the same as that of the child registered most usually (not always) implies illegitimacy. After the letter 'Z' in the births indexes there are listed births where only Christian names were given, often in the case of foundling children. There is a 'Supplementary Index' in the 1984 births index only.

Since the March quarter of 1912 the surname of the spouse is included in the marriage indexes and by searching under this name in the same quarter the forename(s) of the marriage partner can be located under the same reference. Showing the surname of the spouse can be particularly helpful with common surnames and may assist in identifying a particular marriage when otherwise there might be several possibilities.

From the March quarter of 1866 the age of the deceased is shown in the deaths indexes. This can greatly assist in locating a birth entry for an individual, though ages at death are not always accurate. Since the June quarter of 1969 the deaths indexes include the date of birth of the deceased, and no longer their age. Again it may not always be accurate, but is nevertheless a more than useful guide when searching for a possible birth.

Since 1984, when there is only one annual index for each event, the first two figures in the register reference number indicate the month when the event was registered. The above free information does not occur in locally held register office indexes. It should be pointed out that the references in the national births, deaths and marriages indexes for England and Wales have no significance at all in local register offices.

Local Register Offices

Searches in indexes held by local register offices are much less arduous than searching in the national indexes at St Catherine's House, but can only be made by appointment and on payment of a daily 'General Search' fee. Daily general searches in indexes held by local register offices may include up to eight free verifications of information from the registers. Access to information in the registers by the verification system is a service at the discretion of the local superintendent registrar for which there is no statutory provision and therefore may vary considerably from register office to register office. Some register offices may not even allow verifications now. Thus family historians are advised to enquire about the level of information which can be expected from verifications (if any) before making an appointment to check local indexes in register offices. Register offices allowing researchers eight free verifications will require a fee for any further verifications requested in a general search. They cannot be carried out over more than one agreed day, unless a further full search fee is paid, and in some smaller register offices where opening hours are restricted daily searches have to be completed during these times.

HOW TO APPLY FOR ENGLISH AND WELSH CERTIFICATES

Copy certificates of registered events listed in the indexes in either local register offices or in the national indexes must be bought for fees. Certificates are also available at reduced fees for the purpose of certain Acts of Parliament, but none apply to family history research. The cheapest method currently is to apply to a local register office, by post or in person, or to apply in person with the full references from the national indexes at the Family Records Centre in London. The General Register Office operates a fairly costly 'Priority' service in addition to the other methods of purchase outlined below. Priority applications are usually available for collection or despatched within 48 hours of an application.

In person at the Family Records Centre
Certificates applied for after completing application forms (red for births, green for marriages and mauve for deaths) and paying the appropriate fees at the FRC can usually be mailed by first class post to the applicant or collected on the fourth working day after the application was made. From time to time delays occur in producing certificates and you should be advised of these at the tills when processing your application. There are different application forms when applying for other events from the

miscellaneous indexes or 'Overseas' indexes collections (see below under 'Other Records held at the Family Records Centre). You will be asked on the application forms to state the reasons why you are applying for each certificate, and will be requested to furnish extra personal family details when seeking to purchase certificates for more recent events. For the purposes of detection and prevention of crime, information relating to all applications may be passed onto other Government departments or law enforcement agencies. Payments can be made in cash, by credit/debit cards, or by cheques backed up with cheque cards. Cheques should be made payable to 'ONS'.

Reference checking
From the indexes it is not always possible to positively identify an event of interest (particularly so with common names) and there may be several entries which could be the one sought. Additional known details (like the known Christian name(s) of a father in the case of a birth or marriage application) about an event may be entered on the reverse of the certificate application form. If any of them do not agree with the details of the registration applied for a certificate will not be produced and the applicant will receive a part refund of the fee. This service is known as the 'Reference Checking System' and may be used with a 'Reference Checking Sheet' (obtainable from the Customer Services Desk) so that checks can be carried out on a number of different, but possible, entries. Caution should be exercised when using these checking systems as facts can sometimes differ in the actual records from those collected from family or other sources that may lead to misunderstandings. A separate leaflet outlining this service is available.

Postal, telephone, fax, minicom or e-mail applications
The public may also apply for certificates by other methods from the Office for National Statistics. Postal applications should be sent to: Office for National Statistics, General Register Office, PO Box 2, Southport, Merseyside PR8 2JD.

The same office handles telephone applications on 0151-471-4816, faxes on 01704-550013, minicom communications on 0151-471-4530 and e-mail requests on: certificate.services@ons.gov.uk.

The above services must include pre-payment with debit/credit card details required using the technological systems.

If a full national index reference is supplied, the certificate fee is slightly more costly than that paid when making applications in person at the FRC or at a local register office. Certificates applied for with known index references should be despatched within ten working days. A more expensive fee is charged for applications requiring staff to make a three-year search in the indexes to locate an event. This service does not include checking surname spellings or Christian names that may be switched around, etc. Certificates issued when staff have had to locate the event in the indexes for customers are usually despatched within twenty working days. In the event of a negative search only a partial refund will be made. See above under 'In Person at the Family Records Centre' for methods of payment.

Using record agents
Family historians unable to visit the FRC in London often employ record agents to carry out searches and order certificates on their behalf. Agents that offer this type of service in London regularly advertise in commercial and family history societies' magazines.

From Local Register Offices
Certificates may be applied for in person or by post at local register offices for prepaid fees. If you do not know the actual date of the event it is usual for staff to carry out at least a three-year search for the event, centred on the suggested year. Fees for events that cannot be found are refunded in full by local register offices. Searches in indexes held by local register offices may also include alternative spellings of a specified surname by helpful staff. If you visit a local register office it is usual, except in certain circumstances, to be issued with the certificate during your visit. Most postal applications to register offices are despatched within a week or two. All postal requests for certificates must be accompanied by a stamped self-addressed envelope. It is usual to make cheques payable to the 'Superintendent Registrar', but some register offices request payment to their local government authority, and to avoid delay it can be worthwhile to check this out by telephone first. Sometimes finding the correct register office may be a problem as quite a number of the older registration districts with their main register offices have been absorbed into newer ones, abolished or renamed. Staff in your nearest register office should be able to supply you with the addresses and phone numbers of all other

register offices within England and Wales. An alphabetical listing, with addresses, of current English and Welsh register offices also appears in the booklet 'District Register Offices in England and Wales', published by the East Yorkshire Family History Society. A similar listing of English and Welsh register offices, including those abolished and showing the register offices where their records are now deposited, is on the Internet at: www.genuki.org.uk/big/eng/RecOffice

COPIES OF THE GENERAL REGISTER OFFICE NATIONAL INDEXES

Many county record offices, large reference libraries and even some family history societies now have microform (mostly microfiche) copies of the national indexes to civil registration registers. A listing of the major holdings appears in Appendix I at the back of this volume. Copies of the national indexes continue to be sold to various new venues, so it is worthwhile making local enquiries if you fail to find a nearby collection in the appendix, in case of a recent purchase. In addition researchers may find sets (or part sets) of these national indexes in some of the Church of Jesus Christ of Latter-day Saints' Family History Centres (FHCs). Family History Centres are small genealogical research units attached to some, but not all, LDS (Mormon) churches where genealogical research can be undertaken by anyone. You do not have to be a member of the LDS Church to use these facilities. A full list of current UK Family History Centres appears in Appendix II. New FHCs are being set up all the time and it may be worth making local enquiries in case one has recently been added to an LDS Church in your area.

Organisations or individuals can purchase the microfiche indexes in blocks and by event(s) from 1837 to within 12 months of the current year. It is intended to make indexes to events in the registers from 1984 available for purchase on CD-ROM. Telephone 0151-471-4357 for further sales details.

At the time of publication there were no official websites on the Internet with comprehensive listings even remotely approaching the coverage of those in the original volumes, or the filmed copies, of the indexes to the civil registration in England and Wales. However 'FreeBMD' is an on-going Internet project with volunteers supplying various random entries and references (only) taken from the indexes initially for the period 1837–c1900. The actual number of BMD entries in the indexes for this period in England and Wales has been estimated at 100 million and based on this figure the index entries on the website in mid 2000 represented less that 2%. Events can be searched for by name, event, or period. If an event is identified the only information then available is the GRO reference. There is no further access to the actual registration of the event. This website is at: FreeBMD.RootsWeb.com/

OTHER RECORDS HELD AT THE FAMILY RECORDS CENTRE

The Registrar General of England and Wales also has custody of a number of other records or registers and their indexes. Of particular interest to family historians are the records that relate to members of the Armed Forces. These include indexes to Regimental Registers of Births 1761–1924 for events in the UK, but also contain many of serving soldiers abroad. The indexes show the name, place, year of event and regiment and are therefore a useful way of discovering the regiment in which an ancestor served if a particular birth can be positively identified. There are also Army marriage registers, but these are not indexed and the registers cannot be inspected. To locate a soldier's marriage you must know the regiment in which he served, the approximate date and then ask at the enquiry desk to be put in touch with the 'Overseas Section', which may conduct a search. Not all soldiers used regimental chapels and many used civilian churches/chapels for their marriages. Then there are the indexes to the Army Chaplains' Returns of Births, Baptisms, Deaths, Burials and Marriages from 1796 until 1880, which took place abroad. These indexes do not show the regiments in which soldiers served. From 1881 to 1955 there are further indexes to the Army Returns of Births, Deaths and Marriages, similar records for the Royal Air Force servicemen and women from 1920 and a further series of indexes to Service Departments Registers of Births and Marriages 1956–1965, which list Army, Royal Navy and Royal Air Force births and marriages abroad.

There are also indexes of war deaths of all service personnel in the Boer War (1899-1902) and in the First (1914-1921) and Second (1939-1948) World Wars. There are separate indexes for Army officers and other ranks for the two world wars, and separate all ranks indexes for Royal Naval personnel covering both World Wars and for the Royal Air Force (Second World War only). Records of those who died during the First World War when serving in the Royal Flying Corps are included in the Army deaths indexes. And information about service personnel who died in both World Wars (including civilians in WW2) can be obtained from: The Commonwealth War Graves Commission, 2 Marlow Road, Maidenhead, Berkshire SL6 7DX. This information can now be checked out on the Internet at: www.cwgc.org

Amongst other miscellaneous records held at the FRC are Marine Register Index Books to records of Births and Deaths at Sea from 1837 to 1965. These relate to English and Welsh births and deaths on shipping. After 1875 the registers name the ship where the event took place. Similar indexes refer to Air Register Books of Births and Deaths from 1947 to 1965 on civilian aircraft.

Other indexes held include those to the Consular Registers of Births, Deaths and Marriages of British subjects in many foreign countries, registered by British Consuls. They start in 1849 and cover the period to 1965. Deaths were not registered with consuls until 1859 and from 1906 the spouse's name is shown in the marriage indexes and the age of the deceased is shown in the deaths indexes. Indexes to the United Kingdom High Commissioners' records of Births, Deaths and Marriages in many Commonwealth countries are available for 1940–1981 and there is an index to Miscellaneous Foreign Registers of Births, Deaths and Marriages from 1956 to 1965 containing many entries from the Gulf States. A further set of indexes covers Registers of Births, Deaths and Marriages Abroad from 1966 to 1987, service personnel which replaced some of the other indexes and registers mentioned above.

The above are often termed the 'Overseas Collection', and the volume indexes are located in a separate section at the FRC in London. The Overseas Collections of indexes have also been filmed and microfiche copies may be available with many of the filmed copies of the national indexes to ordinary civil registration; see Appendix I. Indexes to the Overseas, Armed Services and Marine Registers are also available at the Public Record Office, Ruskin Avenue, Kew, Richmond, Surrey TW9 4DU (Tel: 020-8876-3444: Website: www.pro.gov.uk/) where admission is by free reader's ticket (you must prove your identity with a driving licence, passport or banker's card).

There are indexes (in yellow volumes) to adoptions since 1927, by the adopted surname only and also held by the Registrar General, but at Southport is an 'Adopted Children's Register' with particulars of adoptions authorised by various court orders in England and Wales since 1 January 1927. Adopted persons seeking their natural birth records may require counselling and should seek guidance on Tel: 0151-471-4361, or e-mail: adoptions@ons.gov.uk

Also maintained are records of Still-Births in England and Wales since 1 July 1927, but copy certificates can only be obtained with the consent of the Registrar General.

Another service available at the Family Records Centre is 'Scottish Link', an on-line computerised connection to the indexes to Scottish births, deaths and marriages since 1855 (see below under 'Section 2. Scotland'), the index to Scottish divorces since 1984, indexes to 1881 and 1891 censuses of Scotland and indexes to Scottish parish registers before 1855. It should be pre-booked at the Scottish Link Desk in half-hour blocks to a maximum of 2 hours for fees. Also available through the Scottish Link Desk are indexes 1922—1993 to births in Northern Ireland, under the above booking arrangements, though there is no charge for this computerised service. Advance booking for either service should be made by telephone on 020-7533-6438.

CERTIFICATES AND SEARCHES

The birth certificate is usually the starting point for most ancestral research. Even if you have no living relations, you can start your research, by obtaining a copy of your own birth certificate and using the information it contains to trace your parents' marriage. Family historians are warned that the cheaper 'short' birth certificate is useless for family history research.

In England and Wales 'full' **birth certificates** remained unchanged in format from 1837 to 1969. The basic information includes when and where a child was born. A timed birth usually, though not always (as it was sometimes a local tradition to time all births especially in the early years of civil registration) implies a multiple birth in England and Wales. Next comes the child's Christian name(s), its sex, the father's full names and occupation (most often left blank if the child was illegitimate), the mother's full names and her maiden surname, prefixed by 'formerly'. If the mother was previously married, her earlier married name might also be shown (if she volunteered the information) prefixed by 'late'. Then comes the name, address and signature or mark of the informant, the date on which the birth was registered and the signature of the registrar. On the extreme right of the birth certificate is a column, nearly always blank, for alterations or changes to Christian names made within twelve months of the date on which the birth was originally registered. The birth registration is then re-indexed. When the parents had been unable to decide upon name(s) for their child it is possible that the birth registration could have been made under 'male' or 'female' followed by the parents' surname in the births indexes. These listings come at the end of all the other entries for a particular surname in the quarterly indexes. However many of the 'male' and 'female' registrations were for children who died shortly after birth and the appropriate death registration should be sought in the deaths indexes at much the same time. Similarly even if you feel you have found the right entry in the births indexes for an ancestor or relation, you should always check in the deaths indexes from the same quarter to ensure the child survived as an infant. Foundlings are listed after the letter 'Z' in each quarterly index.

During the 19th century many children were born before their parents married and as illegitimates should appear in the births indexes under the surname of the mother. If the parents remained unmarried at the time of birth, but had maintained a pretext of being married, then the child will appear as though legitimate under the surname of the father. Registrars did not request the parents' date of marriage when registering births until the *Population Statistics Act of 1938*. This information was required for statistical processing and does not appear on English or Welsh birth certificates. It became extremely popular during the 19th century to use a maiden surname, normally of the mother, the grandmother, and sometimes even a great grandmother, who married into the family, as a second Christian name for children. Sometimes these surnames used as Christian names were of famous people or friends like a godparent. If a child was illegitimate a surname used as a second Christian name was often the surname of the father. This sometimes meant that if the parents did eventually marry the child could change the names around to appear legitimate or drop the mother's maiden surname. In the early years of civil registration in England and Wales many illegitimate births avoided registration, as already mentioned above. A birth certificate with both the mother and father as informants may imply the parents were not married when the child was born. A birth certificate hopefully identifies the parents and enables the researcher to begin the search for their marriage.

English and Welsh **marriage certificates** have remained unchanged since they were introduced in 1837. They show the place and date of the marriage and should indicate whether the ceremony took place by licence, banns or certificate. The full names of both bride and groom are shown together with their respective ages. Sometimes actual ages are not shown and instead it may state 'of full age', 'full age' or even 'FA', meaning over 21 (until 1969 when the age of majority was reduced to 18). The word 'minor' against a marriage partner indicates someone under 21, or since 1969 under 18, years of age. Ages on marriage certificates can be misleading. Family historians must learn to be cautious and not to place too rigid a reliance on ages as they may have been adjusted for various reasons, whilst an age of '21' may mean '21+'.

The marriage certificate also shows the status of both partners being one of 'bachelor', 'spinster', 'widower', 'widow', or 'divorced'. Until the 20th century it was quite unusual to find an occupation for the bride, but that of the groom should always be shown. Also listed are the couple's respective residences. If they both married from the same address it does not always imply they were living together before the marriage. Most often they used the same address to secure residential qualifications and only pay for banns being called in one parish. Residential qualifications were very easy to obtain in a few weeks and because someone was 'of' a certain place or parish on marriage does not necessarily mean they were born there, or even living there. It is also usual to find the fathers of both the bride and groom listed with their respective occupations and the certificate will also show the names of at least two witnesses and how the couple signed, or 'X' marked, the register. The 'signatures' on copy certificates (unless a photocopy of the original register entry) will not be genuine. Relations often acted as witnesses, and it is always worthwhile trying to find out who they were. An unfamiliar female witness is sometimes a married sister, or a cousin and a witness could be a minor of 'credible' age. The information recorded on marriage registers was assumed to be correct, and fabricated information would not have been questioned unless those recording the marriage knew it was untrue.

Marriage certificates in which one partner was illegitimate may contain a fictitious father, though there is often some truth in his Christian name. When a father's name and occupation has been omitted by one partner it usually points to illegitimacy. When both fathers' names and occupations are absent it can be due to lax recording. If a father was dead at the time of the marriage the word 'deceased' may be included, but it was not compulsory to state whether a father was dead or alive, and the lack of the word 'deceased' does not mean that he was alive. When searching in marriage indexes remember that people often juggled their Christian names around, added to them or dropped one given at birth, whilst some people even used a family pet name, or nickname, rather than their given names when they married. Again do remember that local register offices are not usually able to supply marriage certificates unless the date and the building in which the couple married is known with certainty. If you don't know when a couple married or where, then the easiest way is to find references to the marriage in the national indexes for England and Wales and then apply for a copy at the FRC or to the postal applications section at Southport (see above). The ages of the bride and groom and names of their fathers from marriage certificates can be used to locate their respective births.

There is a popular misconception that it is possible to construct a reasonable family tree without ever bothering to search for the deaths of your ancestors. This can be a very serious mistake, especially when dealing with common surnames and forenames, which can frequently lead to the construction of an erroneous family tree.

Some family historians in England and Wales tend to disregard **death certificates** largely because they do not contain much in the way of genealogical information. If you do not bother with the deaths of your ancestors you may miss out on other important events which sometimes follow when a person dies. These include possible newspaper obituaries, funeral and floral tribute reports in the local press and possible probate records like wills or administrations. Moreover if you search for someone's death in the national deaths indexes you will find their age on death entered in the indexes from 1866 and from 1969 their birth date. This information can greatly assist when searching for their birth registration.

Death certificates show where and when a person died, their names in full, their sex and age at death, their occupation, the cause of death and the signature, description and age of the informant, together with the date of the registration and the signature of the registrar. Most often the informant was a close relation. Again ages on death are prone to error. Exact ages were not always known and were sometimes inspired guesswork by informants. Some people, notably seamen lost at sea in the 19th century, had no death registrations, and there have always been some people who just disappeared, or perhaps changed their names and became someone else for one reason or another. The deaths indexes, especially in the 19th century, included many entries for unidentified people who were found dead. These entries are listed in the indexes after the letter 'Z'.

FAILED SEARCHES AND CIVIL REGISTRATION PROBLEMS

All indexes are prone to errors or omissions and the national indexes are no exception, although the occurrence of such defects is fairly minimal. So it is not always the simple matter it should be to find a particular event in the indexes. As already stated up to 15 per cent of all births went unrecorded from 1837 until 1875 and under these circumstances you may be forced to use a census return or the entry in a baptismal register to prove that the birth took place. Marriages were different and if they took place at all they should figure somewhere in the indexes. There should always be two entries, with matching references, for a marriage under the names of both the bride and groom. Very occasionally, through human error when compiling the indexes, the entry for either the bride or groom was omitted.

A major reason for not finding a marriage is that the period covered by the search was too restricted. If a direct ancestor was amongst the younger children in a very large family, the child's parents could have married 20+ years before. Sometimes couples chose not to marry until the first, or a later, child was born, or the first child did not arrive until they had been married for some years. Some couples did not marry because one partner was already married, having left a previous spouse and divorce was almost impossible for ordinary people during the 19th century. Concealing a pretence of marriage was not too difficult in heavily populated urban areas, but was very difficult in rural areas where most people knew each other's business. In Victorian times people often re-married very quickly after the death of a spouse. Working class husbands could not cope with their jobs and looking after their children if their wife died. Similarly working class wives who lost their husbands had to find someone in work to support them and their children very quickly, or face the prospect of resorting to the local workhouse. There is an extremely slender chance that an original quarterly return from a local superintendent registrar to the Registrar General in London was lost in transit and therefore the event will not appear in the national registers or indexes. So the local register office where the event should originally have been recorded should be approached. Some searches fail because of guesswork about people's ages. We know that most people married in their 20s, but there were always a few who left it until later and some much later!

Problems with names
Other searches fail because people stick too rigidly to modern surname spellings. Most surname spellings were not standardised until the early 20th century, so that people's names may easily have been spelt differently in the 19th century. There was fairly widespread illiteracy in working class families in the 19th century, and registrars would write down a name as they thought it should be spelt at that time. This was not always the way it had been spelt the time before. In the 19th century many people's attitudes to those in authority were different, so that even if they knew their name was spelt incorrectly they may not have had the courage to point out the error. There were also some poor clerks around in the 19th century whose handwriting was not easy to read and, coupled with the laborious process of making copies of copies it is hardly surprising that most errors cropped up in the transcription and indexing processes. The Victorian capitals 'L', 'T' and 'S' were sometimes easily confused so that, for example, entries for SAWYER might be indexed under LAWYER. Also the addition of 'e' and 's' to surnames often placed them far from their more accustomed spellings in the indexes. The omission of a letter, like WHITAKER instead of WHITTAKER, also placed many other surnames between the two phonetic variations. If you do not believe this just count the other different surnames which come between these two names in any

modern telephone directory! If your name is STEVENSON today it may have been STEPHENSON years ago, just as people named FAIR, may have been FARE or even PHAYER, and HAUGHTON may have been recorded at ORTON! So as family historians we do have to be flexible with the way our surnames may have been spelt and try to check all likely variations. Christian names can present problems as some people swapped them around, dropped ones they did not like and even added new ones from time to time. As already briefly mentioned, watch out for pet names like Jack being used for John, Bessie for Elizabeth, Sandy for Alexander and Nellie for Ellen, etc. when people married or died.

Multiple references
If you find more than one possibility for a particular event in the national indexes any of which, or none, may be the correct one you should try to eliminate some on the grounds that the event took place in the wrong geographical area. This may not be easy as events were always registered in the place where they occurred. For example, if great grandfather died on holiday in Blackpool, then his death would be registered there and not in Birmingham where he lived and had his business. If you do not know what area a certain registration district covered from the national indexes, you can seek assistance at the enquiry desk in the Family Records Centre. Also displayed at the FRC are maps showing the different registration (and census districts) of England and Wales for 1837-1851, 1852-1946, and 1946-1965. They are a really useful investment. Copies have been produced by and may be bought from The Institute of Heraldic and Genealogical Studies, 80–82 Northgate, Canterbury, Kent CT1 1BA. Send a stamped self-addressed envelope for prices (or check its website: www.ihgs.ac.uk). In very general terms from 1852 to 1946 the larger the volume number in the national indexes (the first number after the registration district) the further away it was from London (e.g. Bethnal Green was 1c, whilst Newcastle upon Tyne was 10b). The volume numbers of Welsh registration districts all begin with the figure '11'.

If you find several possibilities for a particular birth from the indexes, and know the name of the father at least, or other details about the parents, then it may be better to check each one out at the register office where each different birth was first registered, until you are supplied with the correct certificate. Local register offices refund the cost of the certificate in full if the details of a registration do not agree with the known particulars supplied. A more costly alternative is to use the 'Reference Checking System' at the FRC (see above). If you fail to locate a particular event it is usually a good idea to double check the indexes concerned. Sometimes we may overlook or miss an entry through a sudden lapse in concentration, or because one index volume was not on the shelf at the time and we forgot to backtrack to check it later.

SECTION 2
Scotland

Civil registration began in Scotland on 1 January 1855, following the *1854 Registration Act*. The Scottish authorities initially introduced a very ambitious system that recorded a great wealth of genealogical information when registering births, deaths and marriages. But it was cumbersome to operate and after only one year (1855) the amount of information recorded was reduced to more basic details. Family historians with ancestors in Scotland will discover a great deal about their family if they can find an event which was registered in 1855 and it is always worthwhile looking to see if someone else in an ancestor's family was born, died or married in 1855, as the genealogical detail recorded about the family was so great. The extent of the genealogical information recorded in 1855, and in the subsequent years, is outlined below under 'Scottish Certificates'. From 1856 until 1860 the information recorded was diluted, but from 1861 onwards the levels of genealogical information were improved, but not restored to their 1855 peak. Despite these modifications the Scottish system of civil registration is still the most informative of all the British systems. It is also probably worth noting the time-scales for registering events in Scotland. Births had to be registered within 21 days, deaths within 8 days and marriages within 3 days.

As in England and Wales, Scottish events were originally registered in local register offices in the control of district registrars. At the end of each calendar year district registrars despatched the details recorded to the Registrar General for Scotland in Edinburgh, where they were nationally recorded and indexed by event in annual alphabetical volumes. If your ancestors came from Scotland you are advised to concentrate on these records in Edinburgh, where a computerised index system for locating events (some 42 million statutory index entries to Scottish births, marriage, deaths and divorces) is available. Nowadays there are also copies of the computerised Scottish indexes available at other locations. See below in *Via the Internet,* under 'Obtaining Scottish Certificates' and under 'Copies of New Register House Indexes'.

NEW REGISTER HOUSE

The national registers and indexes, in the custody of the Registrar General for Scotland, are deposited at the General Register Office for Scotland, New Register House, Edinburgh EH1 3YT (Tel: 0131-334 0380 and Fax 0131-314 4400). New Register House is at the east end of Princes Street, directly opposite the Balmoral Hotel and a few minutes walk from the Waverley Railway Station, the bus station and the airport bus stop. There are no facilities for car parking at New Register House, although there are public car parks fairly close. Smoking, eating and drinking are totally banned throughout New Register House (including the toilet areas) as are all ink pens, and biros. Only pencils can be used when making notes. The use of mobile phones is banned in the building and there are no power sockets available for using, or recharging, personal electronic equipment. Self-powered and silent laptop computers may be used. Research amenities at New Register House, connected with the statutory records of civil registration, mean it is possible on a full daily visit to research several generations of a particular family. This is because once an event has been located in the computerised indexes researchers are allowed to see the actual register entry on microfiche, as a privilege (but not a right), and so avoid the necessity of having to purchase unseen certificates, which is a time-consuming and delaying feature of other British systems.

Booking arrangements
The General Register Office for Scotland, New Register House, Edinburgh, is open to the general public on weekdays from 9.00am to 4.30pm. It is closed at weekends and on public holidays. Access is not available to anyone under 16 years of age and people with large personal items of hand baggage or backpacks may also be denied admission. Admission to see all the records held is by valid pass for which a fee must be paid. Passes may be purchased for part of a day, a full day, one week, four weeks, one quarter or one year. Each pass admits only one person; it cannot be shared. Passes, once issued, are not transferable to anyone else and may be withdrawn in cases where the house rules are breached. People with mobility problems, advised in advance, may be given permission to have someone to assist them who is allowed free admission.

Advance bookings can be made for a proportion of the 100 available research places, the remainder are filled on a 'first-comes-first-served' daily basis (depending on the day, a few places may be available at a discounted price), but these are often quickly taken. A special discounted 'Apex' advance-purchase pass is usually available for a limited number of research places, although New Register House reserves the right to reduce or withdraw the numbers of Apex places at busy times. Apex places are sold on a 'first-comes-first-served' basis and bookings open six weeks in advance of a visit. To take advantage of the Apex price researchers need to make a firm booking for a particular day, and pay the whole daily fee fourteen days in advance. Apex bookings can only be made by phone (Tel: 0131-314-4433), or in person at the public counter on normal weekdays from 2.00pm to 4.00pm. Apex payments by phone can be made by credit card (Switch, Visa or MasterCard), or in person by credit card, cheque (supported by a British cheque card) or cash. As Apex places are limited researchers should be prepared to consider alternative dates in case their chosen date is already fully booked. New Register House cannot accept Apex bookings by post, fax or e-mail. Cancellations of Apex places made before 10.00am on the day of the planned visit, will result in a credit being made available towards the cost of a full-price pass on another date within six months of the original reservation. New Register House cannot make cash refunds for cancellations of Apex places. Researchers booked at the Apex rate who do not turn up or contact New Register House before 10.00am on their booked day, are likely to find their place has been allocated to another researcher and no refund or credit is payable in these cases.

Family historians are urged to book in advance of a visit, particularly if travelling any distance, to avoid a frustrating wait in the daily queues that sometimes form for unbooked or cancelled places. Advance bookings for ordinary passes (other than Apex places), including block bookings, can be done in writing (with a stamped self-addressed envelope, by e-mail (record@gro-scotland.gov.uk), by telephone (0131-314-4433), by fax (0131-314-4400), or in person. No advance bookings can be made for part-day research. Ordinary booked places are held over for an hour until 10.00am, unless a later arrival time has been notified. Researchers with weekly (or longer) passes, who cannot get into work on a specified day, or days, covered by their pass are advised to tell the supervisor so that their research place can be allocated to someone else in their absence.

COMPUTERISED INDEXES AND FREE INFORMATION

Until the early 1990s researchers used various paper indexes to Scottish births, deaths and marriages, in heavily bound volumes, to locate a particular entry. This old, time-consuming and tiring method of tracing individual entries has now been replaced with a modern user-friendly computerised system that includes all the 'free' information available in the old index volumes. These include mother's maiden surname (m.s.) in the births indexes since 1929, surname of the spouse in the marriages indexes also since 1929, the age of the deceased in the deaths indexes since 1866 and the maiden surname of the deceased's mother in the deaths indexes since 1974. The female marriage indexes include the surname of the groom from 1855 to 1863 and from 1929 to date, but the male marriage indexes include the surname of the bride only since 1929. Under Scottish law women do not lose their maiden surnames on marriage and the indexes in New Register House have always reflected this. Thus women appear twice in the marriage indexes (more if married more than once) under their maiden surname and their married surname and from 1859 married women appear twice (or more) in the deaths indexes under both surnames, unless the maiden surname was unknown to the informant. Deaths of step or illegitimate children may be indexed under both original and later, or assumed, surnames.

The computerised alphabetical indexes all include the parish or registration district where the event was originally registered and the entry number in the appropriate register. Using the computerised terminals to search for a particular event, researchers are prompted to enter certain details about each person sought. This information is typed into the computer via a standard keyboard. Some of the keys are in different colours to make the instructions easier to follow. Researchers are asked to identify the event being sought (birth, death or marriage), the sex of the person, the year of the event and their surname and initial letter of their first forename (not the full forename). When these details have been supplied the computer begins its search and displays, on the monitor, those entries which most nearly match. There are often several possibilities, sometimes with common surnames more than one full screen of entries, but many of them will be eliminated through having an incorrect forename, or being in the wrong registration district. Other information, like the maiden surname of the mother in the case of a birth (only since 1929), or the name of the spouse in the case of a marriage, will assist with the process of selecting the correct entry. If the event does not occur in the selected year, the computer will prompt the researcher to try the previous or following year, and so on.

The computer can also check out spelling variations that sound similar, in case the event was registered under an unexpected spelling. Researchers who have difficulty in operating the terminals can seek instruction in using the equipment, but not individual research help, from members of staff. Once an event is identified from the computerised index the full reference should be noted on an order slip and taken to the self-service storage area where copies of the registers are available on microfiche. Unsupervised self-service access is allowed and the appropriate microfiche should be withdrawn and replaced in its exact position by the completed order slip. The microfiche containing the entry can then be taken to the researcher's reader where the actual register entry can be inspected. Researchers are not allowed to remove more than three microfiche at any one visit to the self-service storage area, and they should not replace their microfiche after use, but put them in the appropriate re-filing trays for replacement by the staff. If a particular microfiche is not in its place when required, the completed order slip should be placed in the appropriate tray so that staff can later bring it to the researcher, after it has been returned from someone else for re-filing. Researchers are asked not to 'browse' through the registers. Access to these filmed records is a privilege allowed by New Register House, as statutory rights extend only to seeing the indexes and to buying copies of the certificates. However under this special concession researchers are allowed to make pencil notes, if required, from the filmed registers. Certified register copies may be ordered for fees during a visit when in possession of a valid pass. They may be collected or can be posted within five working days. Much cheaper uncertified photocopies of pages from birth or marriage registers from 1855 to 1899, or death registers from 1855 to 1924 (and only from these years) can also be ordered up to 15 minutes before closure on the same day during a visit.

OBTAINING SCOTTISH CERTIFICATES

In person, by post or by fax

All certificate orders must be prepaid. Not all family historians are able to pay a visit themselves to New Register House, and others may not wish to make a general search for, perhaps, just one certificate during a visit. Under these circumstances New Register House staff can make what is called a 'Particular Search' for a specified event after applications by post, telephone, fax, or in person (not by e-mail). Each search can only cover up to five years (usually the year quoted and the two preceding and two following years). Particular search fees for applications in person are slightly cheaper than those applied for by other means (as above). Additional fees (document fees) are charged for birth, death or marriage certificates produced as a result of particular searches with or without the five-year search. Certificates applied for in person are normally posted off or ready for collection within five working days. Payments in person at New Register House, or by post, may be made in cash, by sterling cheque with cheque card, by credit card (Switch, Visa, and MasterCard) or by traveller's cheque. Cheques or postal orders should be made payable to 'The Registrar General'. Postal applications can also be paid by credit card, but all orders by telephone (0131-314-4411) or fax (0131-314-4400) must be paid by credit card only. Fax applications including credit card payment should be accompanied by the card holder's signature as it appears on the card. All postal or faxed orders are normally despatched within ten working days of the application and remittance being received at New Register House. A more costly 'Priority Service' is available to provide certificates usually on the working day following application.

Via the internet (Scots ORIGINS)

You can now search the Scottish national indexes to the Statutory Registers of births and marriages from 1855-1899 and deaths from 1855 to 1924 and order certificates from these periods via the Internet by using Scots ORIGINS at: www.origins.net/

Containing in mid-2000 around 30 million names (including births and marriages in Scottish Old Parish Registers 1553–1854, and the 1891 Scottish Census Index, the 1881 Scottish Census Index will be available later in 2000) the Scots ORIGINS database is one of the world's largest genealogical sites and further expansion is expected. There is a modest fee payable by credit card to access the database once on-line, which provides 30 'page credits' (permission to download 30 pages of record entries containing a maximum of 15 entries each) over a period of 24 hours since making the payment. The indexes on the Internet are searchable by various different fields, including event, names, year of event, registration district and in the case of marriages by the spouse's name. The website contains full information on how to make searches, including a full demonstration, descriptions of the kind of information to be found in the indexes, a list of 'Frequently Asked Questions' and contact e-mail addresses if problems occur.

Ordering a certificate (often called a register entry) can be done on-line by paying a further fixed fee by credit card and the system automatically transfers the request to the General Register Office for Scotland to fulfil the order and mail the document to you within fifteen working days. Researchers concerned about using credit cards on this service have an assurance that the service is more secure than using a credit card (for example) in a restaurant and details are transferred from web browsers in encrypted form for authorisation by your card issuer. No credit card numbers are held anywhere on the system.

Using record agents
For more complicated searches outside the parameters of general or particular searches or the coverage of the Internet indexes, or for people unable to visit Edinburgh, New Register House can supply a list of professional researchers, or record agents, who will undertake searches in the statutory records on your behalf in return for fees. The Registrar General takes no responsibility whatever for the quality, or value for money, of work done by any researcher in this listing.

From Scottish Register Offices
It is also possible to obtain Scottish certificates from local register offices in Scotland, but you must know with certainty where and approximately when an event was first registered. Applications for certificates may be made in person or by post to local register offices for fees. Researchers may also visit local register offices to carry out a 'General Search' in their local indexes of events, but not in the registers. General Searches in a Scottish local register office's indexes must be prepaid per agreed session, and can only be made by appointment. Certificates can be ordered in local

register offices for events identified in either the local or national indexes. A listing of current Scottish register offices and their addresses appears in 'The Parishes, Registers & Registrars of Scotland', published by the Scottish Association of Family History Societies (ISBN 1-874722-05-6). Addresses and telephone numbers may also be obtained from any Scottish register office. A Directory of Registrars in Scotland, including office addresses and telephone numbers is on an Internet website at: wood.ccta.gov.uk/grosweb/grosweb.nsf/pages/file1/$file/reglist.pdf

COPIES OF NEW REGISTER HOUSE INDEXES

At a number of Scottish Registration Offices it is also possible, by appointment and for fees, to access the same computerised indexes to Scottish births, deaths and marriages since 1855 as those held at New Register House in Edinburgh. They are as follows:

Aberdeen: Registrars' Office, St Nicholas House, Upperkirkgate, Aberdeen AB10 1EY (Tel: 01224-522616).

Ayr: Sandgate House, 43 Sandgate, Ayr KA7 1DA (Tel: 01292-284988).

Cupar: County Buildings, St Catherine Street, Cupar, Fife KY15 4TD (Tel: 01334-412200).

Dumfries: Municipal Chambers, Buccleuch Street, Dumfries DG1 2AD (Tel: 01387-245906).

Dundee: 89 Commercial Street, Dundee DD1 2AG (Tel: 01382-435222).

Elgin: 240 High Street, Elgin, Moray IV30 1BA (Tel: 01343-554600).

Glasgow: 22 Park Circus, Glasgow G3 6BE (Tel: 0141-287-8364/8350).

Inverness: Farraline Park, Inverness IV1 1NH (Tel: 01463-239792).

Lerwick: County Buildings, Lerwick, Shetland ZE1 0HD (Tel: 01595-744562).

Lochgilphead: Dalriada House, Lochnell Street, Lochgilphead PA31 8ST (Tel: 01546-604511).

Stornoway: Town Hall, 2 Cromwell Street, Stornoway, Isle of Lewis HS1 2DB (Tel: 01851-709438).

These offices all charge different fees for searching in the computerised indexes and it is advisable to ascertain these when making an appointment in advance of a visit. In Scotland the computerised New Register Houses indexes are not available outside the Scottish Registration Service.

In England these Scottish indexes are also available via a computer link at the Family Records Centre, 1 Myddelton Street, London EC1R 1UW (Tel: 020-8392-5300). It is called 'Scottish Link' and provides access to the indexes in half-hour blocks for a maximum of two hours per person on payment of fees. Booking in advance of a visit is advisable (Tel: 020-7533-6438). For details of the content of Scottish Link at FRC see 'Section 1. England and Wales' (above) under 'Other Records held at the Family Records Centre'.

Researchers are also reminded that Scots ORIGINS on the Internet allows access to the older computerised civil registration indexes for Scotland (see *Via the internet*, above under 'Obtaining Scottish Certificates) at: www.origins.net/

Filmed copies of the old paper index volumes are available in some UK (see Appendix II) and overseas Family History Centres (FHCs) attached to some, but not all, Churches of Jesus Christ of Latter-day Saints. You are advised to check with individual FHCs as not all centres have the Scottish indexes. Alternatively, where FHCs do not have the Scottish indexes available, it may be possible for staff to order filmed copies spanning a given period for a nominal fee.

The Society of Genealogists (SoG), 14 Charterhouse Buildings, Goswell Road, London EC1M 7BA (Tel: 020-7251-8799; Website: www.sog.org.uk) has microfilm copies of these indexes covering the years 1855–1920, as well as the actual register entries for the year of 1855 only. Admission to SoG is by membership or by payment of daily/hourly fees for non-members.

OTHER RECORDS HELD AT NEW REGISTER HOUSE

Other records of interest to family historians at New Register House include Old Parish Registers covering some 900 Scottish parishes for the years 1553–1854 (indexes computerised and also on the internet at Scots ORIGINS, see above) and a complete set of all the Scottish decennial Census Enumerators' Transcripts Books (census returns) for 1841, 1851, 1861, 1871, 1881 and 1891. The census returns after 1891 remain confidential, though those for 1901 will become available in January 2002. There is an index to the 1891 Scottish census on Scots ORIGINS on the Internet (and the Scottish index to the 1881 census should be added during 2000). The

1881 census for Scotland is also already indexed and transcripts are available on the CD-ROMs produced by the Church of Jesus Christ of Latter-day Saints.

Amongst other statutory records are Registers of Still-Births in Scotland, since 1939, which are closed to the general public except in exceptional circumstances, and an 'Adopted Children Register', since 1930, under orders made by Scottish Courts. Also there is a Register of Scottish Divorces, since May 1984 with computerised index, showing the names of the parties, the date and place of the marriage, the date and place of the divorce and details of orders made by the court regarding the custody or financial provision for the children.

There are Marine Registers of Births and Deaths since 1855 and Air Registers of Births and Deaths, from 1948, on British-registered shipping or aircraft in any part of the world, when one of a child's parents was Scottish, or if a deceased person was usually resident in Scotland.

Armed Forces service records date from 1881 and include Army Returns of births, deaths and marriages of Scottish persons at military stations abroad during the period 1881–1959. Service Department Registers cover the period since 1959 with details of service births, deaths and marriages outside the UK which relate to Scottish persons serving in HM Armed Forces, whilst Army Chaplains' Marriages list marriages of Scottish personnel outside the UK since 1892. There are registers of war deaths of Scottish persons serving in the Boer War (1899–1902), World War I (1914–1918) and World War II (1939–1945). Again Scottish deaths in both world wars can be checked out with the Commonwealth War Graves Commission (full details above, under 'Other records held at the Family Records Centre') or on its website at www.cwgc.org

Consular returns of births, deaths and marriages since 1914 relate to persons of Scottish descent or birth, and similar records kept by High Commissioners in certain Commonwealth Countries, concerning Scottish persons, date from 1964. Finally there are Births, Deaths and Marriages registers of Scottish people in Foreign Countries from 1860 to 1965, based on information supplied by the parties, and a register of Foreign Marriages of Scottish persons in certain foreign countries since 1947. A more comprehensive listing of these records is available by sending a stamped self-addressed envelope to New Register House and requesting a copy of the 'List of Main Records in the care of the Registrar General'.

SCOTTISH CERTIFICATES

As stated certificates for events registered in 1855 in Scotland, the first year of civil registration, are particularly informative. Thereafter Scottish certificates contain less detail, but are still the most informative of all the different British certificates. Never buy 'short' Scottish birth certificates as they are useless for family history research.

'Full' Scottish **birth certificates** contain the full names of the child and its sex, the date and time of birth (all Scottish birth registrations are timed), the address where the birth occurred, and the father's full names and occupation. The names of the mother are also shown, including her maiden surname (m.s.) and any previous married names. The date and place of the parents' marriage (not recorded on certificates between 1856 and 1860) is shown together with the name and address of the informant and their relationship to the child (if any). Finally the date on which the birth was registered is recorded plus the signature of the registrar. An 1855 version will also show the ages and birthplaces of both parents, plus details of other children (number and sex, and if alive or dead, but not their names) born prior to the 1855 birth registration.

Scottish **marriage certificates** show the date and place of the marriage, the type of ceremony (there were no civil ceremonies until 1939) if by proclamation or consent, the full names, ages (not always accurate and discontinued from 1972), signatures, marital status, usual addresses, and occupations, if any, of both the bride and groom. Also recorded are the full names and occupations of both fathers, and the full names of both mothers, including their maiden surnames. It was usual for deceased parents to be listed as such. The certificate is completed by the names of the witnesses and the name of the officiating minister (or registrar from 1940) in the case of regular marriages. For irregular marriages certificates should include the date of conviction (to 1939) or the decree of Declaration of Marriage or Sheriff's warrant. Most irregular marriages took place according to the form of the Established Church, but were performed without banns (proclamation), or were marriages by consent (abolished in 1939) and the parties applied to a local Sheriff's Court for Registration. They were regarded as clandestine but were perfectly valid. From 1855-1922 any relationship between the bride and groom was also shown on certificates. The 1855 marriage certificate also shows the place of birth and date of registration of the bride and groom with details of any previous marriages, including numbers of children from any such marriage(s) and if these children were living or deceased. From 1864 the addresses of witnesses are also included and from1972 the date and county of birth of both parties is again shown. Very occasionally copies of Scottish marriage certificates do not show the Christian names of the bride and groom, and they are replaced by initials. This is usually because the couple signed their names with initials instead of their full Christian names in the original marriage record, and in the process of copying the entry for the national records, and initials have been substituted. The full Christian names can usually be found in the original marriage record. Sometimes in such cases, the indexes include the full Christian names, but the copy certificate supplied only shows initials.

From 1855 until 1984 **Scottish divorces** were noted on the marriage entry in the register by writing 'Divorce Register of Corrected Entries' (often abbreviated to 'Divorce RCE'). There is no index to these divorces and they can only be located by checking the marriage register entries. This practice was largely discontinued in mid 1984 and New Register House has a separate computerised index to Scottish divorces after 1 May 1984 and can supply details of extracts for fees. These extracts from the registers include names of the parties, dates and place of marriage, date and place of the divorce and details of any order made by the court regarding financial provision for any children. The computerised divorce index since 1984 can be seen at the Family Records Centre, London, for a modest fee via 'Scottish Link'.

Scottish **death certificates** are the most informative of all the British death certificates. They show the full names of the deceased person, their sex and age, the date, time and place of death, and their usual abode if different from the place of death. They list occupations and marital status, which usually includes the name of any spouse or previous spouse(s). Names of spouses are not included on registrations made from 1856 to 1860. The cause of death, any duration of disease and the name of the medical attendant (if any) are also shown. Of particular interest to family historians are the full names of the deceased's parents, including the mother's maiden surname and whether either parent is deceased. The documentation is completed with the signature and relationship to the deceased (if any) of the informant and their address (though not in 1855), when the death was registered and the signature of the registrar. Extra details on death registrations made in 1855 are the birthplace of the deceased, how long they lived in the district before death, and the full names and ages of any alive or dead children. Also listed was the burial place and name of the undertaker, which was continued until 1861. Scottish death certificates show the date of birth of the deceased from 1967.

Northern Ireland and The Republic of Ireland

Civil registration of non-Catholic marriages began in Ireland on 1 April 1845, but full statutory registration of all births, deaths and marriages did not start throughout the whole of Ireland until 1 January 1864. It is known that some events after 1864, particularly births and marriages, went unrecorded in Ireland. Some estimates suggest as many as 15 per cent of Irish births and marriages were never registered, especially in the early years. The Irish system of state registration was based on the catchment areas of public health districts that in turn were divisions within the old Poor Law Unions with a communal workhouse. These districts were known as 'Registration Districts', each in the control of a superintendent registrar. Registration districts were subdivided into smaller areas known as 'Registrar's Districts' (or 'Dispensary Districts') where local registrars, responsible to their superintendent registrars, collected the registrations of events within each district. Until 1922 these were collated and indexed and details passed on to the Registrar General for Ireland, at the General Register Office in Dublin, where national master indexes and registers for the entire country were produced.

Two Systems

In 1922 Ireland was divided into Northern Ireland and the Irish Free State. Northern Ireland comprised the six north-eastern counties of Antrim, Armagh, Down, Fermanagh, Londonderry and Tyrone. The Irish Free State comprised the remaining 26 counties of Ireland being Carlow, Cavan, Clare, Cork, Donegal, Dublin, Galway, Kerry, Kildare, Kilkenny, Laois, Leitrim, Limerick, Longford, Louth, Mayo, Meath, Offaly, Monaghan, Roscommon, Sligo, Tipperary, Waterford, Westmeath, Wexford and Wicklow. The Irish Free State adopted the name of Eire under its 1937 constitution and did not become the Republic of Ireland until 1949, at which point it left the (British) Commonwealth. This division of Ireland in 1922 means that separate systems of civil registration have been conducted from that date in both Northern Ireland and in what is now the Republic of Ireland.

Irish Names

In the early years of Irish civil registration there can be many variations in surname spellings and researchers are advised to prepare for possible alternative spellings. The popular Irish surname prefix of 'O' was regarded by some registrars as optional until the end of the 19th century so, for example, an event for an O'KELLY may have been registered under KELLY. Similarly surnames beginning with 'Mac' may easily appear under 'Mc'. There can be problems, too, with the forenames as sometimes people with two or more forenames were only registered with one, which was most often their first forename. With common surnames this can present real problems in identifying one individual from a number of possibilities. If the precise location where an event took place is known it is sometimes worth considering an approach to the local register office where the event should have been registered and seeking to obtain a copy certificate there. Register office staff can sometimes be very helpful and addresses of local Irish register offices can be found in Irish regional telephone directories under 'Health Board'.

REGISTERS AND INDEXES

All Ireland pre-1922 and post-1922 Republic of Ireland

It is important to establish in which part of Ireland your ancestors lived. The Registrar General, General Register Office, Joyce House, 8-11 Lombard Street East, Dublin 2, Republic of Ireland (Tel: 00-3531-6711000) has custody of indexes and copy registers relating to births and deaths in any part of Ireland from 1 January 1864 to 31 December 1921 and in the Irish Free State, Eire or the Republic of Ireland from 1 January 1922 to date. General Register Office, Dublin, also has the indexes and registers to the non-Catholic marriages of all denominations from 1 April 1845 to 31 December 1863, all Irish marriages from 1 January 1864 to 31 December 1921 and marriages in the Irish Free State, Eire or Republic of Ireland from 1 January 1922 to date.

46

Northern Ireland

If your ancestors lived in one of the six counties making up Northern Ireland then some of the registers of interest will be in the custody of the Registrar General for Northern Ireland, Northern Ireland Statistics & Research Agency, General Register House, Oxford House, 49-55 Chichester Street, Belfast BT1 4HL, Northern Ireland (Tel: 028-90-252021/22/23/24). Held here are birth and death registration records for the Northern Ireland counties from 1 January 1864 to date, but registrations of marriages in Northern Ireland go back only to 1 January 1922. Oxford House has indexes to the Northern Ireland birth registrations since 1864, but only has indexes to Northern Ireland death and marriage registrations since 1 January 1922. If you seek a marriage in Northern Ireland before 1922, then the best place to locate it is in the all-Ireland marriage registrations and indexes held in Dublin at Joyce House (see above), or in the marriage registrations from 1845 to 1921 held by registrars in local district register offices (see section below *From Register Offices* under 'Obtaining Irish Certificates'). To trace death entries between 1864 and 1921 at Oxford House the registration district must be known.

To sum up, if you need to locate an event in Northern Ireland since 1922 (or a birth from 1864) then the easiest method is to approach Oxford House in Belfast. For events before 1922 in Northern Ireland (except births) and in any part of the rest of Ireland since 1864 (or since 1845 for non-Catholic marriages) then the easiest method is to approach Joyce House in Dublin.

Index volumes

Irish indexes are in annual alphabetical volumes by category of events from 1864 to 1877 and in four quarterly volumes for each year from 1878 to 1973. From 1903 to 1927 inclusive the births indexes (only) revert back to one annual volume and from this year also show the maiden surname of the mother against each birth registration. Births indexes from 1903 also include the actual date of birth until 1921 in Northern Ireland and until 1928 in the Republic of Ireland. Marriages are indexed twice under the names of the bride and groom. Deaths indexes also contain the age of the deceased, which may be inaccurate. Within each alphabetical index volume events are listed by surname, forename(s), the registration district where it took place and the volume and page number of the register in which it was recorded. Retrospective or late registrations were possible in Ireland because of the numbers of events that slipped through the administrative net. They do not appear in the indexes in the year in which the event was late-registered, but are to be found in the year in which the event originally took place. In the case of births and deaths late registrations are listed separately at the back of the appropriate births or deaths index volume. Late registrations for marriages are added to the main marriages indexes in the appropriate year and alphabetical place, together with the normal marriage entries.

OBTAINING IRISH CERTIFICATES

The general public has a right of access to the various Irish national indexes, but no right to see the Irish registers, at both Dublin and Belfast. To discover details of an entry in the registers copy certificates must be bought.

From Dublin

The General Register Office at Joyce House in Dublin is open to the public on normal weekdays Monday to Friday 9.30 am to 12.30 pm and 2.15 pm to 4.30 pm, but closed at weekends and on public holidays. Appointments are not really necessary and casual visitors can usually be accommodated. There are two daily fee-paying searches available to visitors that must be prepaid. A relatively inexpensive 'Particular Search' allows access to any five years of the indexes for one particular event only. Thus researchers looking for two separate events like a marriage followed by a birth, would be required to make two separate searches and pay two 'Particular Search' fees. The more expensive 'General Search' allows unlimited access to the birth and death indexes during a period not exceeding six hours, or unlimited access to the marriage indexes on any number of successive days not exceeding six. The cost of copy certificates when an event is found, whether the less expensive uncertified printouts or the more costly certified copies (if authentification of a register entry is required), is additional in both forms of search. This service is only available to visitors to Joyce House.

Certificates can be ordered by post for fees if the year and full index reference is known. If these details are not known and researchers require staff to carry out a search in the indexes for an event there is an increased fee for the certificate. Index-searches by Joyce House staff cannot cover more than five years and are usually the suggested year and the two preceding and two following years. Postal applications should include as many known facts as possible about an event. All applications for certificates must be prepaid and cheques or money orders made payable to 'The Registrar General'. Sterling and other currencies are not legal tender in the Republic of Ireland, but sterling cheques drawn on UK banks are acceptable as are USA dollar payments. International Reply Coupons (available from post offices) should be enclosed to cover return postage from Dublin, unless you live in the Republic of Ireland.

From Belfast
The indexes held by the Registrar General for Northern Ireland, at Oxford House in Belfast are also open for inspection by the general public. Oxford House is open on normal weekdays from 9.30 am to 4.00 pm, but is closed at weekends and on public holidays. Visitors should be aged 16 or over. Admission is by reservation (booking is advisable and necessary for 'Assisted Searches', see below) and on payment of different fees. For a modest fee per person a search, not exceeding five years, can be made in the indexes for one nominated event. A more expensive daily fee per person allows for searches not exceeding six hours in duration with access to all the indexes for all three events. This service includes four verifications from the registers with an option to others on payment of a further fee per verification. Finally there is a rather more costly hourly fee for an 'Assisted Search' by a member of the GRO staff. This service also includes verifications being read out from the actual registers and it is advisable to book this latter service at least six months in advance, unless cancellations have occurred. Occasionally unbooked daily visitors can be accommodated for unassisted searches, but it is always advisable to book all research places in advance. Costs of certificates are additional to the fees paid for searches in the indexes. Oxford House can also handle pre-paid postal requests for certificates that can include a five-year search in the indexes, but they are more expensive than postal requests when the year and full reference from the indexes are known. Cheques, etc, should

be made payable to 'The Registrar General' and crossed. Payments may also be made by certain credit cards. Self-addressed stamped envelopes or two International Reply coupons should be included with all postal requests for return postage. Certificates ordered on visits are usually processed in three working days and those by post within eight workings days of receipt. NB Cheaper printouts of certificates (as in Dublin) are not available in Belfast, only full certified copies.

From Register Offices
Copies of Irish certificates can also be bought for fees from superintendent registrars at local, or 'District', register offices in both the Republic of Ireland and Northern Ireland. However researchers need to know the district where an event took place to approach the correct office.

But beware; in Northern Ireland whilst register offices can supply historic copy marriage certificates, they can only supply copy birth and death certificates for events registered there within the last three years. Postal applications must include the appropriate fee and a self-addressed stamped envelope from mainland Britain or two International Reply Coupons for return postage if from elsewhere. The Belfast Registry, City Hall, Belfast (Tel: 028-9032-0202) should be able to supply details of specific register offices throughout Northern Ireland. Local register offices in Northern Ireland are also listed on the Internet on the General Register Office (Northern Ireland) website under 'District Council Registration Offices' at: www.nisra.uk/gro/

And in the Republic of Ireland although register offices can meet requests for historic birth and death certificates, they can only produce historic copy certificates for Catholic marriages. Postal applications from outside the Republic must include the appropriate fee and include two International Reply Coupons for return postage. A detailed listing of Superintendent Registrars' Offices in the Republic of Ireland appears in 'Appendix B' of, *Civil Registration of Births, Deaths and Marriages in Ireland: A Practical Approach*, by Catherine Blumson (Ulster Historical Foundation). A listing of registrars offices or County Superintendent Registrars Offices in the Republic of Ireland is on the Internet at: www.groireland.ie/fees.htm

COPIES OF THE IRISH INDEXES
AND SOME EARLY IRISH REGISTERS

Copies of the Irish births, deaths and marriages indexes, and sometimes 19th century filmed copies of the actual registers (though far from all), are available in some Family History Centres attached to Churches of Jesus Christ of Latter-day Saints (see Appendix II). For example Hyde Park (London) Family History Centre has filmed indexes for births and deaths from 1864 until 1949 and marriages from 1845 until 1949, whilst Belfast FHC, in addition to copies of the indexes, has filmed copies of the actual registers for births from 1864 to 1880 and 1900 to 1913, marriages from 1845 to 1870 and deaths from 1864 to 1870.

The Family Records Centre, 1 Myddelton Street, London EC1R 1UW has computerised indexes of births in Northern Ireland from 1922-1993. It is free to use and must be booked at the 'Scottish Link' desk in half-hour blocks. Telephone for advance bookings (Tel: 020-7533-6438).

Also do not forget to check out the International Genealogical Index (IGI) for Ireland. The 1992 microfiche edition, and subsequent CD-ROM versions (which can be seen at Family History Centres, etc), are particularly good for abbreviated entries of Irish births registered in 1864, 1865, 1866 and the later 1860s. The 'Vital Records Index − British Isles' (BIVRI) is also worth consulting. It also contains a number of abbreviated entries of Irish births 1865-1874 and Irish non-Catholic marriages 1847-1864. The BIVRI is available for sale on CD-ROM from the Church of Jesus Christ of Latter-day Saints, The Distribution Centre, 399 Garretts Green Lane, Birmingham B33 0UH (Tel: 0121-785-2200). It should also be available to search (not for sale) at LDS Church Family History Centres.

OTHER RECORDS HELD IN DUBLIN AND BELFAST

Both Registrars General in Dublin and Belfast have other records and registers about Irish people that may be of interest to family historians. At Joyce House, Dublin, there are registers of births and deaths at sea from 1864-1921 for all Ireland and from 1922 for the Republic of Ireland. There are registers of births and deaths of Irish people abroad certified by British Consuls from 1864-1921 and marriages at the German Protestant Church, Dublin from 1806 to 1837 (known as 'The Schulze Register').

There are various Army births, deaths and marriages recorded under the *Army Act of 1879*, an Adopted Children Register since 1953 and other registers which relate to Irish people outside Ireland, including a register of certain Irish people with Lourdes Marriages since 1972. A full list of these records is available from Joyce House on an information sheet. With the authorities in Northern Ireland at Oxford House, Belfast, are an 'Adopted Children Register' from 1931, Births and Deaths at Sea from 1922, Consular and High Commissioners' records of Births, Deaths and Marriages of Northern Ireland people abroad since 1922, Service Department Registers from 1927, World War II Armed Forces Deaths (1939–1948), etc.

IRISH CERTIFICATES

Irish civil registration certificates contain similar information to those for England and Wales. Copy certificates from the General Register Offices in Dublin or Belfast do not contain any original signatures. Irish **birth certificates** show the date and place of birth, the name(s) of the child and its sex, the names of the father and his address and occupation, the names of the mother including her maiden surname, the date the birth was registered and particulars of the informant together with their signature and the signature of the registrar.

Irish **marriage certificates** list the place and type of ceremony, together with the registration district or Poor Law Union and county where it took place and the date of the marriage and whether by banns or licence. Particulars recorded about the bride and groom include their full names, their marital status (bachelor, spinster, widower or widow), their ages (although sometimes only shown as 'of full age', meaning over 21), their addresses, and the names of their respective fathers and their occupations. The occupation of the groom is shown though seldom one for the bride until fairly recent times. Marriage certificates also show how the couple signed the register and include the name, signature of the official who carried out the ceremony and the names and signatures of at least two witnesses - often close relatives or friends.

Although **death certificates** generally do not contain much helpful genealogical information, they should not be ignored as sometimes details given (like an age) can be used to locate other events. The Irish death certificate shows the date and place of death, the name and age of the deceased, their sex and 'condition' (marital status), occupation (if any), the certified cause of death, the duration of any final illness and usually the name of a medical practitioner who certified the death. The date the death was registered and the name of the informant is shown, and this was usually a relation, together with their signature and that of the registrar who recorded the death.

SECTION 4

The Isle of Man

Compulsory civil registration of births and deaths began on the Isle of Man in 1878, and marriages followed in 1884 (some non-compulsory births and marriages from 1849 - see below). The indexes and registers are in the custody of the Head of Registries, General Registry, Registries Building, Deemsters' Walk, Bucks Road, Douglas, Isle of Man IM1 3AR (Tel: 01624-687039). Researchers can visit the General Registry and have free access to filmed copies of the annual index volumes for each event from 9.00 am to 1.00 pm and 2.00pm to 5.00pm on normal weekdays. The registry is closed at weekends, on bank holidays and annual TT Race week in July. Advance warning of a visit is not essential and most casual visitors can usually be accommodated. The use of laptop computers is allowed. Isle of Man copy certificates can be supplied for applications in person or by post for fees and are usually ready for collection the same day or the day following the application. Searches in the indexes can be undertaken for postal applications by staff, for an additional fee for each year searched. Such search fees are additional to the cost of the certificate. All fees must be prepaid. When writing to the General Registry cheques and/or money orders should be made payable to 'The Isle of Man Government' and if you cannot obtain Manx postage stamps always include two International Reply Coupons. **The Isle of Man certificates contain the same information as those for England and Wales**. Filmed copies of the indexes to the Isle of Man civil registration registers from 1878 to date are also held at Manx National Heritage Library, Manx Museum and National Trust, Douglas, Isle of Man IM1 3LY (Tel: 01624-648001). Opening hours 10.00am to 5.00pm on normal weekdays and Saturdays.

The Head of Registries also holds a number of other important Isle of Man records of interest to family historians. These included an 'Adopted Children Register' begun in 1928 (not open for public inspection, though birth certificates can be issued in respect of children who have been adopted under the *Adoption Acts*), filmed copies of many baptismal, marriage and burial registers for Anglican parishes on the island from circa 1600 to circa 1877/78, and some filmed nonconformist registers (many indexed), mainly from the beginning of the 19th century. It may be worth noting that until 1849 Isle of Man nonconformists were required by law to marry in Anglican churches and non-compulsory marriage certificates were issued from 1849 for dissenters who married in nonconformist churches or chapels in the presence of a Deputy Registrar. Similarly there may be some non-compulsory birth certificates from 1849. Family historians with ancestry on the island are advised to join the Isle of Man Family History Society, 3-5 Atholl Street, Peel, Isle of Man IM5 1HG. (Website: www.isle-of-man.com/interests/genealogy/fhs/).

SECTION 5

The Channel Islands

The Channel Islands have always operated their own independent systems of civil registration and they remain quite separate from those on the British mainland. Each of the main islands runs its own system with varying starting dates and coverage of events.

On **Jersey** civil registration began in August 1842 and births and deaths were recorded in the island's twelve parishes by parish registrars. Copies of these registers are held by: The Superintendent Registrar, 10 Royal Square, St Helier, Jersey JE2 4WA, Channel Islands (Tel: 01534-502335). Normal weekday office hours are 9.30am to 12.30pm. Marriage registers are kept in the parishes by the clergy, but the Registrar General also has records of all marriages on the island, including civil ceremonies since 1842, or when a particular marriage register was started. There are normally no facilities for visitors to carry out their own research at Royal Square, although due to a recent relaxation of the regulations there is limited access to the registers, by appointment only, from 9.00am to 11.00am Monday to Friday. Certificates can be supplied to visitors who call in.

Postal enquiries and applications for certificates should be sent to the Superintendent Registrar at the above address. All applications for certificates must be prepaid and the fees for certificates usually include a five-year search in the indexes. In addition postal charges must be prepaid and researchers are advised to establish the full costs before sending in their applications and remittances. Cheques or money orders in sterling should be made payable to 'The Treasurer of the States'. **Jersey certificates** follow the pattern of those on mainland England, but the Jersey marriage certificate usually gives the place of birth of both the bride and the groom, which can be useful. Copies of the indexes from 1842 to 1900 are also available at the Société Jersiaise, 7 Pier Road, St Helier, Jersey JE2 4XW, Channel Islands (Website: www.societe-jersiaise.org), and at the Channel Islands Family History Society Research Room (see below for details of CIFHS). Many families on Jersey are of French extraction and initially they may have chosen to register their family events with the French Consulate on Jersey from 1842. An 'Adoption Register' was begun on Jersey in 1948. When corresponding with the authorities on Jersey remember to include two International Reply Coupons as the island has its own postal stamps and mainland UK or overseas stamps are not acceptable as return postage.

Civil registration began on **Guernsey, Jethou and Herm** in 1840. The registers and indexes to them are in the custody of HM Greffier, General Register Office, The Greffe, Royal Court House, St Peter Port, Guernsey GY1 2PB, Channel Islands (Tel: 01481-725277). Normal weekday office hours are 9.00am to 5.00pm. Births, deaths and marriages on the islands of **Sark and Alderney** have only been centrally registered on Guernsey since 1925 as well as on the islands themselves. Searches at Royal Court House may be made in the indexes only and on payment of a nominal admission fee per person per visit. From 2.00pm to 4.00pm daily the Strong Room is open and fee-paying visitors can copy down details from the actual records. Each register is indexed separately on an island-wide basis, except for deaths before 1963 that are indexed by the parish where they occurred. Deaths of married women before 1949 are indexed under their maiden surnames only and Church of England and many Roman Catholic marriages before 1919 were not registered, and so should be sought in the appropriate parish marriage register. Copies of birth, death and marriage certificates must be bought for pre-paid fees. Staff can undertake a five-year search in the indexes for postal queries for specific events and provide a certificate for fees. Cheques should be made payable to 'The Registrar General'. Other basic records of interest to family historians at the General Register Office on Guernsey include wills of real property, available census records for Guernsey, Alderney and Sark with indexes, some Quaker records, some early Anglican parish registers, and various First and Second World War records, including births, marriages and deaths of Guernsey inhabitants evacuated to England or interned in Germany. There are filmed copies of many of the Guernsey civil registration indexes also available at The Priaulx Library, Candie Road, St Peter Port, Guernsey, Channel Islands (Tel: 01481-721998; Website: user.itl.net/~glen/priaulx.html) which is open Mondays to Saturdays 9.30 am to 5.00 pm.

Guernsey **birth and marriage certificates** are almost identical to the English and Welsh certificates. However the Guernsey **death certificates** are more informative. The additional details are the name of any spouse, a place of birth since 1907 and the names of the parents, including the maiden surname of the mother. Before 1907 they usually include a time of death. Like the other Channel Islands Guernsey issues its own postage stamps and International Reply Coupons should be included to cover the cost of return postage when writing to the authorities.

Researchers with ancestors on **Alderney** requiring information on civil registration events since it began there, with births and deaths in 1850 and marriages from 1886 and since 1925 (as an alternative to Guernsey) should contact: The Greffier, Registry for Births, Deaths, Companies, Land and Marriages, St Anne, Alderney GY9 3AA, Channel Islands, (Tel: 01481-822817). Fees as per Guernsey with cheques made payable to 'The States of Alderney'. Researchers should note that there are some gaps in these early Alderney registers, ie deaths registers 1875-1907 are missing, etc.

Similar information about civil registration on **Sark** before and since 1925 (only deaths were registered, and these only since 1915) may be obtained from: The Greffier, Greffe Office, Sark GY9 0SF, Channel Islands (Tel: 01481-832012). Fees as per Guernsey with cheques payable to 'The Inhabitants of Sark'.

It is understood the only copies of any of the Channel Islands civil registration indexes, outside the Channel Islands themselves, are those for Guernsey 1842-1969 which are held at the Society of Genealogists, 14 Charterhouse Buildings, Goswell Road, London EC1M 7BA (Tel: 020-7251-8799; Website: www.sog.org.uk), where admission is by membership or by payment of daily/hourly fees for non-members. There is also a chance that some Channel Islanders' families may figure in the listing of births, deaths and marriages in the Miscellaneous Foreign Returns 1831-1958 (RG 32, indexed in RG 43) held at the Public Record Office, Ruskin Avenue, Kew, Richmond, Surrey TW9 4DU (Tel: 020-8876-3444; Website: www.pro.gov.uk/). A number of Channel Islanders' events may appear amongst the births and marriages entries on the International Genealogical Index (IGI) which is always worth checking. A great deal of research work, including extensive indexing projects (mainly of parish registers and Channel Islands' families), has been accomplished by the Channel Islands Family History Society and researchers with ancestry on any of the Channel Islands should consider contacting the Secretary for further details. The address of the CIFHS is PO Box 507, St Helier, Jersey JE4 5TN (Website: user.itl.met/~glen/AbouttheChannelIslandsFHS.html). There is also a Family History Section of the Société Guernesiaise, PO Box 314, Candie, St Peter Port, Guernsey GY1 3TG, Channel Islands (Website: user.itl.net/~glen/fhssocguer.html)

QUICK REFERENCE

Civil Registration Addresses

England and Wales
The Registrar General, Office for National Statistics, General Register Office (England and Wales), Smedley Hydro, Trafalgar Road, Birkdale, Southport PR8 2HH (Tel: 0151-471-4800)
Website: www.statistics.gov.uk
Postal Application Section, Office for National Statistics, General Register Office, PO Box 2, Southport, Merseyside PR8 2JD (Tel: 0151-471-4816, Fax: 01704-550013)
E-mail: certificate.services@ons.gov.uk
Website: www.statistics.gov.uk/registration
Family Records Centre, 1 Myddelton Street, London EC1R 1UW (Tel: 020-8392-5300)
Website: www.open.gov.uk/register/frc.htm

Scotland
The Registrar General for Scotland, General Register Office for Scotland, New Register House, Edinburgh EH1 3YT, Scotland
(Tel: 0131-334 0380 or to reserve a research place 0131-314-4433; Fax 0131-314 4400)
E-mail: record@gro-scotland.gov.
Website: www.gro-scotland.gov.uk
Scots ORIGINS website: www.origins.net

Northern Ireland
The Registrar General for Northern Ireland, Northern Ireland Statistics and Research Agency, General Register Office, Oxford House, 49–55 Chichester Street, Belfast BT1 4HL, Northern Ireland
(Tel: 028-90-252021/2/3/4/5)
E-mail: gro.nics@dfpni.gov.uk
Website: www.nisra.gov.uk/

Republic of Ireland
The Registrar General, General Register Office, Joyce House,
8–11 Lombard Street East, Dublin 2, Republic of Ireland
(Tel: 00-3531-6711000)
(Oifig An Ard-Chlaraitheora, Teach Sheoighe, 8–11 Sraid Lombaird
Thoir, Baile Atha Cliath 2)
E-mail: Via Website (on 'Contact Us')
Website:www.groireland.ie/

Isle of Man
The Head of Registries, Civil Registry, Registries Building, Deemsters'
Walk, Bucks Road, Douglas, Isle of Man IM1 3AR (Tel: 01624-687039)
E-mail: civil@registry.gov.im
Website: www.gov.im/

Channel Islands

Alderney (BD from 1850 and M from 1886)
The Greffier, Registry for Births, Deaths, Companies, Land and
Marriages, St Anne, Alderney GY9 3AA (Tel: 01481-822817)

Guernsey (including Jethou and Herm, but Alderney and Sark only
from 1925)
HM Greffier, General Register Office, The Greffe, Royal Court House,
St Peter Port, Guernsey GY1 2PB, Channel Islands (Tel: 01481-725277).

Jersey
The Superintendent Registrar, 10 Royal Square, St Helier, Jersey JE2
4WA, Channel Islands (Tel: 01534-502335)

Sark (pre-1925 only deaths were registered, and these only since 1915)
The Greffier, Greffe Office, Sark GY9 0SF, Channel Islands
(Tel: 01481-832012)

Other Useful Addresses Mentioned

Channel Islands Family History Society, PO Box 507, St Helier, Jersey
JE4 5TN, Channel Islands
Website: user.itl.met/~glen/AbouttheChannelIslandsFHS.html
Commonwealth War Graves Commission, 2 Marlow Road, Maidenhead,
Berkshire SL6 7DX.
Website: www.cwgc.org
Institute of Heraldic and Genealogical Studies, 80–82 Northgate,
Canterbury, Kent CT1 1BA
Website: www.ihgs.ac.uk
Isle of Man Family History Society, 3–5 Atholl Street, Peel, Isle of Man
IM5 1HG
Website: www.isle-of-man.com/interests/genealogy/fhs/
Manx National Heritage Library, Manx Museum and National Trust,
Douglas, Isle of Man IM1 3LY (Tel: 01624-648001)
Priaulx Library, Candie Road, St Peter Port, Guernsey, Channel Islands
(Tel: 01481-721998)
Website: user.itl.net/~glen/priaulx.html
Public Record Office, Ruskin Avenue, Kew, Richmond, Surrey TW9
4DU (Tel: 020-8876-3444)
Website: www.pro.gov.uk/
Société Jersiaise, 7 Pier Road, St Helier, Jersey JE2 4XW, Channel
Islands
Website: www.societe-jersiaise.org
Société Guernesiaise (Family History Section), PO Box 314, Candie, St
Peter Port, Guernsey GY1 3TG, Channel Islands
Website: user.itl.net/~glen/fhssocguer.html
Society of Genealogists, 14 Charterhouse Buildings, Goswell Road,
London EC1M 7BA (Tel: 020-7251-8799)
Website: www.sog.org.uk

Internet Sites Mentioned

Local register office listings with addresses and telephone numbers, etc

England and Wales
www.genuki.org.uk/big/eng/RecOffice

Scotland
wood.ccta.gov.uk/grosweb/grosweb.nsf/pages/file1/$file/reglist.pdf

Northern Ireland
(Under General Register Office, then under District Council Registration Offices)
www.nisra.uk/gov/

Republic of Ireland
www.groireland.ie/fees.htm

Other useful websites relating to civil registration matters, etc

FamilySearch
(IGI, Ancestral File, LDS Family History Centres, etc)
www.familysearch.org

FreeBMD
(Scant unofficial England and Wales civil registration indexes)
FreeBMD.RootsWeb.com/

Genuki
(Not mentioned in text, but contains extensive information pages about British genealogical sources, family history societies, websites, register offices, etc)
www.genuki.org.uk/

Index of places in each English or Welsh registration district
www.genuki.org.uk/big/eng/civreg/places/

Registration districts in England and Wales,1837–1930 (by county and parishes in each RD)
www.fhsc.org.uk/genuki/reg

Scots ORIGINS
(Official Scottish national indexes BM 1855–1899 and D 1855–1924 with certificate ordering facilities, plus indexes to Scottish 1891 census (1881 Scottish census indexes added during 2000), and indexes to Scottish parish registers 1553–1854)
www.origins.net

APPENDIX I

MICROFORM COPIES OF THE REGISTRAR GENERAL'S NATIONAL INDEXES OF BIRTHS, DEATHS AND MARRIAGES (BDM) FOR ENGLAND AND WALES HELD BY LOCAL AUTHORITIES OR OTHER ORGANISATIONS

Researchers are advised to check on the actual period covered by the filmed holdings of the BDM indexes at a particular venue. ALWAYS BOOK IN ADVANCE of a visit as at some centres there may be a waiting list. Nearly all of the listed holdings cover the 19th century and the early to mid-20th century BDM indexes, some to the 1990s. Holdings may be in microfilm or microfiche format. You may find it helpful to take along a magnifying glass. Some venues may only allow researchers a certain length of time to search in the indexes. A Reader's Ticket may be required at some places and you may have to prove your identity with a passport, driving licence or similar. You may also be expected to pay a small fee to view the indexes at some places. This list excludes organisations that require a substantial fee or do not wish their details to be published.

NB. ADDITIONAL COPIES OF THESE INDEXES ARE BECOMING AVAILABLE AT DIFFERENT LIBRARIES AND COUNTY RECORD OFFICES ALL THE TIME, SO RESEARCHERS WITHOUT LISTED COPIES ACCESSIBLE NEARBY ARE ADVISED TO CHECK AND SEE WHETHER ANY NEW HOLDINGS HAVE RECENTLY BEEN ADDED AT LOCAL REPOSITORIES.

ENGLAND

BEDFORDSHIRE
Bedford Central Library, Harpur Street, Bedford MK40 1PG
  (Tel: 01234-350931)

BERKSHIRE
Berkshire Record Office, 9 Coley Avenue, Reading RG1 6AF
  (Tel: 0118-9015132)

BRISTOL
Bristol Central Library, College Green, Bristol BS1 5TL
(Tel: 0117-9299147)

BUCKINGHAMSHIRE
County Reference Library, Walton Street, Aylesbury HP20 1UU
(Tel: 01296-382250)

CAMBRIDGESHIRE
County Record Office Cambridge, Shire Hall, Castle Street, Cambridge
CB3 0AP (Tel: 01223-717281)

CLEVELAND
Middlesbrough Central Library, Victoria Square, Middlesbrough
TS1 2AY (Tel: 01642-263359)

CORNWALL
Cornish Studies Library, 2–4 Clinton Road, Redruth TR15 2QE
(Tel: 01209-216760)
Cornwall Family History Society Library, 5 Victoria Square, Truro
TR1 2RS (Tel: 01872-223797)

CUMBRIA
Carlisle Library, 11 Globe Lane, Carlisle CA3 8NX (Tel: 01228-607321)

DERBYSHIRE
Derbyshire Family History Society, Bridge Chapel House,
St Mary's Bridge, Sowter Road, Derby DE1 3AT
Derbyshire Local Studies Library, County Hall, Matlock DE4 3AG
(Tel: 01629-585579)

DEVON
Devon Family History Society, Units 3B & 4B 7/9 King Street, Exeter
North Devon Record Office, Tuly Street, Barnstaple EX31 1EL
(Tel: 01271-388607)

DORSET
Dorset Record Office, 9 Bridport Road, Dorchester DT1 1RP
(Tel: 01305-250550)

DURHAM
Darlington Library, Crown Street, Darlington DL1 1ND
   (Tel: 01325-462034)

ESSEX (see also LONDON)
Essex Society for Family History's Research Room, c/o Essex Record
   Office (Ground Floor), Wharf Road, Chelmsford CM2 6YT
   (Tel: 01245-244644)

HAMPSHIRE
Hampshire Record Office, Sussex Street, Winchester SO23 8TH
   (Tel: 01962-846154)
Portsmouth County Library, Guildhall Square, Portsmouth PO1 2DX
   (Tel: 023-9281-9311 ext 232 or 234)

HEREFORDSHIRE
Hereford Record Office, The Old Barracks, Harold Street, Hereford
   HR1 2QX (Tel: 01432-265441)

HERTFORDSHIRE
Hertfordshire Archives and Local Studies, County Hall, Hertford
   SG13 8EJ (Tel: 01992-555105)

ISLE OF WIGHT
Isle of Wight County Library, Lord Louis Library, Orchard Street,
   Newport PO30 1LL (Tel: 01963-823800)

KENT (see also LONDON)
The Institute of Heraldic and Genealogical Studies, Northgate,
   Canterbury CT1 1BA (Tel: 01227-768664)

LANCASHIRE (including Merseyside and Greater Manchester)
Bolton Archives and Local Studies, Central Library, Civic Centre,
   Bolton BL1 1SE (Tel: 01204-522311)
Crosby Library, Local History Unit, Crosby Road, North, Waterloo,
   Liverpool L22 0LQ (0151-928-6487)
Liverpool Record Office, Central Library, William Brown Street,
   Liverpool L3 8EW (Tel: 0151-225-5417)
Greater Manchester County Record Office, 56 Marshall Street,
   New Cross, Manchester M4 5FU (Tel: 0161-832-5284)
Huyton Library, Civic Way, Knowsley L36 9GD (Tel: 0151-443-3738)

Preston District Library and Local Studies, Harris Library,
Market Square, Preston PR1 2PP (Tel: 01772-404000)
St Helens Local History and Archives Library, Central Library, Gamble
Institute, Victoria Square, St Helens WA10 1DY (Tel: 01744-456952)
Stockport Archive Service, Central Library, Wellington Road, South,
Stockport SK1 3RS (Tel: 0161-4744530)

LINCOLNSHIRE
Lincolnshire Archives, St Rumbold Street, Lincoln LN2 5AB
(Tel: 01522-525158)

LEICESTERSHIRE
Leicestershire and Rutland Family History Society's Research Centre,
Freeschool Lane, Leicester (Tel: 0116-2516567)

LONDON
London Borough of Bromley, Local Studies and Archives Section,
Central Library, High Street, Bromley, Kent BR1 1EX (Tel: 0208-460
9955 ext 261)
London Borough of Havering, Reference and Information Library,
St Edward's Way, Romford, Essex RM1 3AR (Tel: 01708-772394)
London Borough of Greenwich, Greenwich Local History and Archives,
Woodland, 90 Mycenae Road, Blackheath, London SE3 7SE
(Tel: 0208-858-4631)
London Borough of Harrow, Harrow Reference Library, Civic Centre,
Station Road, Harrow, Middlesex HA1 2UU (Tel: 0208-424-1056)
London Borough of Redbridge, Local History Library, Clements Road,
Ilford, Essex IG1 1EA (Tel: 0208-4787145 ext 225)
Society of Genealogists, 14 Charterhouse Buildings, Goswell Road,
London EC1M 7BA (Tel: 020-7251-8799). Entrance by membership or
fee for non-members

MIDDLESEX (see LONDON)

MIDLANDS, WEST
Birmingham City Archives, Central Library, Chamberlain Square,
Birmingham B3 3HQ (Tel: 0121-303-4549)
Archives and Local History Service (Dudley MBC),
Mount Pleasant Street, Coseley, West Midlands WV14 9JR
(Tel: 01384-812770)

Coventry Central Library, Smithford Way, Coventry CV1 1FY
(Tel: 024-7682-2366)
Sandwell Community History and Archives, Smethwick Library,
High Street, Smethwick, Warley, West Midlands B66 1AB
(Tel: 0121-558-2561)
Walsall Local History Centre, Essex Street, Walsall, West Midlands
WS2 7AS (Tel: 01922-721305)
Wolverhampton Archives and Local Studies, 42–50 Snow Hill,
Wolverhampton WV2 4AG (Tel: 01902-552480)

NORFOLK
Norwich Local Studies Library, Gildengate House (2nd Floor),
Anglia Road, Norwich NR3 1AX (Tel: 01603-215254)

NORTHUMBERLAND
Berwick-upon-Tweed Record Office, Council Offices, Wallace Green,
Berwick-upon-Tweed TD15 1ED (Tel: 01289-330044 ext 230)
Morpeth Records Centre, The Kylins, Loansdean, Morpeth NE61 2EQ
(Tel: 01670-504084)

NOTTINGHAMSHIRE
Nottinghamshire Family History Society, 10 Lyme Park, West Bridgford,
Nottingham NG2 7TR
Church of Jesus Christ of Latter-day Saints, Stanhope Square,
West Bridgford, Nottingham NG2 7GF (Tel: 0115-9144255)

OXFORDSHIRE
Centre for Oxfordshire Studies, Central Library, Westgate, Oxford
OX1 1DJ (Tel: 01865-815749)

SOMERSET
Bath Central Library, 19 The Podium, Northgate Street, Bath BA1 5AN
(Tel: 01225-428144)
The Church of Jesus Christ of Latter-day Saints, Forest Hill, Yeovil
(Tel: 01935 426817)

STAFFORDSHIRE (see also MIDLANDS, WEST)
Staffordshire Record Office, Eastgate Street, Stafford ST16 2LZ
(Tel: 01785-278372)

SUFFOLK
The Research Room, Orwell High Street, Maidstone Road, Felixstowe IP11 9E

SUSSEX (EAST AND WEST)
Brighton Reference Library, Church Street, Brighton BN1 1UE (Tel: 01273-296969)
Worthing Library, Richmond Road, Worthing BN11 1HD (Tel: 01903-212060)

TYNE AND WEAR
Newcastle upon Tyne Heritage Information Centre, City Library, Princess Square, Newcastle upon Tyne NE99 1DX (Tel: 0191-261 0691)
Northumberland and Durham Family History Society, Bolbec Hall (2nd Floor), Westgate Road, Newcastle-upon-Tyne NE1 1SE (Tel: 0191-261-2159)
South Tyneside Central Library, Prince George Square, South Shields NE33 2PE (Tel: 0191-4271818 ext 2135)
Sunderland City Library and Arts Centre, 28–30 Fawcett Street, Sunderland SR1 1RE (Tel: 0191-5148439)

WILTSHIRE
County Local Studies Library, Trowbridge Reference Library, By the Sea Road, Trowbridge BA14 8BS (Tel: 01225-713732)

WORCESTERSHIRE
Worcestershire Record Office, County Hall, Spetchley Road, Worcester WR5 2NP (Tel: 01905-766351)

YORKSHIRE
East Riding Archive Office, County Hall, Beverley HU17 9BA (Tel: 01482-885007)
West Yorkshire Archives, Kirklees Central Library, Princess Alexandra Walk, Huddersfield HD1 2SU (Tel: 01484-221965)
Hull City Archives, Central Library, Albion Street, Hull HU1 3TF (Tel: 01482-615102)
Local Studies Library, Leeds Central Library (2nd Floor), Calverley Street, Leeds LS1 3AB (Tel: 0113-2478290)

Northallerton Library, 1 Thirsk Road, Northallerton DL6 1PT
  (Tel: 01609-776271)
Sheffield Archives, 52 Shoreham Street, Sheffield S1 4SP
  (Tel: 0114-2734756)
York Library, The Reference Library, Museum Street, York YO1 2DS
  (Tel: 01904-655631 ext 37/38)

WALES
Bridgend Library and Information Service, Coed Parc, Park Street,
  Bridgend CF31 4BA (Tel: 01656-767451)
Carmarthenshire Archive Service, County Hall, Carmarthen SA31 1JD
  (Tel: 01267-234567)
Church of Jesus Christ of Latter-day Saints, Heol y Deri, Rhiwbina,
  Cardiff (Tel: 029-2062-5342)
Denbighshire Record Office, 46 Clwyd Street, Ruthin LL15 1HP
  (Tel: 01824-708250)
Flintshire Reference and Information Service, Library HQ, County Hall,
  Mold CH7 6NW (Tel: 01352-704411)
Glamorgan Record Office, Glamorgan Building, King Edward VII
  Avenue, Cathays Park, Cardiff CF1 3NE (Tel: 029-2078-0282)
National Library of Wales, Dept of Manuscripts and Records,
  Aberystwyth, Ceredigion SY23 3BU (Tel: 01970-632800)
Newport Libraries, Reference Library, John Frost Square, Newport
  NP9 1PA (Tel: 01633-211376)
West Glamorgan Archive Service, County Hall, Oystermouth Road,
  Swansea SA1 3SN (Tel: 01792-636589)

SCOTLAND
Aberdeen and North East Scotland Family History Society,
  164 King Street, Aberdeen AB24 5BD (Tel: 01224-646323)
General Register Office for Scotland, New Register House, Edinburgh
  EH1 3YT (Tel: 0131-334-0380)

AUSTRALIA★

Australia's Immigration and Family History Centre, Natureworld, Corner Fairway Drive/Mayborough Road, Pralba, Hervey Bay, Queensland 4655

Australian Genealogical Education Centre, Railway Parade, Kiama, New South Wales 2533

Australian Institute of Genealogical Studies, 1/41 Railway Road, Blackburn, Victoria 3130. (View by membership or entrance fee.)

Genealogical Society of Queensland, First Floor, Corner Hubert/Stanley Streets, Woolloongabba, Queensland 4102

Genealogical Society of Tasmania Inc, 2 Taylor Street, Invermay, Launceston, Tasmania 7250

Genealogical Society of Tasmania Inc (Branch Libraries) PO Box 60, Prospect, Tasmania

Genealogical Society of Victoria, 179 Queen Street, Melbourne, Victoria 3000

Mayborough Family Heritage Institute Inc, 210 Lennox Street, Mayborough, Queensland 4650

Griffith Genealogical and Historical Centre, Tranter Place, Griffith, New South Wales 2680

Heraldry and Genealogy Society of Canberra Inc, GPO Box 585, Canberra, ACT 2601. (View by membership.)

National Library of Australia, Newspaper and Microcopy Room, Canberra, ACT 2607

Perth Cultural Centre, Alexander Library Building, Perth, Western Australia 6000

Playford City Local and Family History Centre, 3 Windsor Square, Elizabeth, South Australia 5112

Queensland Family History Society Inc, Old Albion Fire Station, 42 Bridge Street, Albion, Brisbane, Queensland 4068

Richmond-Tweed Family History Society, Research Room, PO Box 817, Ballina, New South Wales 2478

Salisbury Public Library Service, Len Beadell Library, 55 John Street, Salisbury, South Australia 5108

★ Denotes that other holdings of microformed copies of the Registrar General's BDM indexes for England and Wales are probably also now available in these countries.

Society of Australian Genealogists' Library, 24 Kent Street, Sydney,
New South Wales 2000
South Australia Genealogy and Heraldry Society Inc, 201 Unley Road,
Unley, South Australia 5061
Victoria State Library, Genealogy Centre, 328 Swanston Street,
Melbourne, Victoria 3000

CANADA★
Calgary Family History Centre, 2021-17th Avenue SW, Calgary, Alberta,
Canada
Campbell River Genealogy Club, St John's Building,
170 Dogwood Street, Campbell River, British Columbia
Saskatchewan Genealogical Society, 201–1870 Lorne Street, Regina,
Saskatchewan, SP4 3E1

NEW ZEALAND★
Auckland Research Centre, Auckland City Libraries, Lorne Street,
Auckland
Porirua Public Library, 4 Norrie and Parumoana Streets, Porirua

UNITED STATES OF AMERICA★
Krans-Buckland Family Association Office, 6505-34th Street,
North Highlands, California 95660, USA
Genealogical Society of Utah, Family History Library,
35 North West Temple, Salt Lake City, Utah 84150, USA

Family History Centres

Family History Centres are small genealogical research units attached to some, but not all, Churches of Jesus Christ of Latter-day Saints throughout the world. For small fees it is possible to order any filmed records which the LDS Church has, like census returns and many parish registers. Some also have filmed copies of the indexes to births, deaths and marriages for the different British systems of civil registration. The listing below shows the Family History Centres in the British Isles at the start of 2000. The LDS Church continues to open new Family History Centres. Family History Centres are manned by volunteers and are only open at specified times which vary from Centre to Centre. You should always make an appointment before any visit. Listings of Family History Centres can also be seen on the internet (under custon search) on: www.familysearch.org

NB Addresses are mailing addresses only and because of limited staffing Family Records Centres cannot respond to any mailed enquiries.

ENGLAND

BEDFORDSHIRE
St Albans FHC, Corner of London Road/Cutenhoe Road, Luton, LU1 3NQ
(Tel: 01582-482234)

BERKSHIRE
Reading FHC, 280 The Meadway, Tilehurst, Reading, RG3 4PF
(Tel: 01189-410211)

BRISTOL
Bristol FHC, 721 Wells Road, Whitchurch, Bristol BS14 9HU
(Tel: 01275-838326)

BUCKINGHAMSHIRE
High Wycombe FHC, 743 London Road, High Wycombe
(Tel: 01494-459979)

CAMBRIDGESHIRE
Cambridge FHC, 670 Cherry Hinton Road, Cambridge CB1 4DR
(Tel: 01223-247010)
Peterborough FHC, Cottesmore Close, Off Atherstone Avenue,
Netherton Estate, Peterborough (Tel: 01733-263374)

CLEVELAND
Billingham FHC, The Linkway, Billingham, TS23 3HG
(Tel: 01642-563162)

CORNWALL
Helston FHC, Clodgey Lane, Helston (Tel: 01326-564503)
St Austell FHC, Kingfisher Drive, St Austell (Tel: 01726-69912)

CUMBRIA
Barrow FHC, Abbey Road, Barrow-in-Furness (Tel: 01229-820050)
Carlisle FHC, Langrigg Road, Morton Park, Carlisle CA2 5HT
(Tel: 01228-526767)

DEVON
Exeter FHC, Wonford Road/Barrack Road, Exeter (Tel: 01392-250723)
Plymouth FHC, Hartley Chapel, Mannamead Road, Plymouth
(Tel: 01752-668666)

DORSET
Poole FHC, 8 Mount Road, Parkstone, Poole BH14 0QW
(Tel: 01202-730646)

ESSEX
Romford FHC, 64 Butts Green Road, Hornchurch RM11 2JJ
(Tel: 01708-620727)

GLOUCESTERSHIRE
Cheltenham FHC, Thirlestaine Road, Cheltenham (Tel: 01242-523433)
Forest of Dean FHC, Wynol's Hill, Queensway, Coleford
(Tel: 01594-832904)
Yate FHC, Wellington Road, Yate, (Tel: 01454-323004)

HAMPSHIRE
Aldershot FHC, LDS Chapel, St Georges Road, Aldershot
(Tel: 01252-321460)
Portsmouth FHC, Kingston Crescent, Portsmouth (Tel: 023-9269-6243)

HEREFORDSHIRE
Hereford FHC, 262 Kings Acre Road, Hereford (Tel: 01432-265775)

HERTFORDSHIRE
Stevenage FHC, Buckthorne Avenue, Stevenage (Tel: 01438-351553)
Watford FHC, Hempstead Road, Watford (Tel: 01923-251471)

ISLE OF MAN
Douglas FHC, Woodside, Woodbourne Road, Douglas
(Tel: 01624-675834)

ISLE OF WIGHT
Newport FHC, Chestnut Close, Shide Road, Newport (Tel: 01983-529643)

KENT
Canterbury FHC, Forty Acre Road, Canterbury (Tel: 01227-765431)
Gillingham FHC, 2 Twydale Lane, Gillingham
Maidstone FHC, 76b London Road, Maidstone ME16 0DR (Tel: 01622-757811)
Orpington FHC, Station Approach, Orpington (Tel: 01689-837342)

LANCASHIRE (including GREATER MANCHESTER and MERSEYSIDE)
Ashton FHC, Patterdale Road, Ashton under Lyne, Lancashire
(Tel: 0161-330-3453)
Birkenhead FHC, Prenton Lane/Reservoir Road, Prenton, Birkenhead
(Tel: 0151-608-7723)
Blackpool FHC, Warren Drive, Cleveleys, Blackpool FY5 3TG
(Tel: 01253-858218)
Chorley FHC (see below under Preston Temple FHC)
Lancaster FHC, Overangle Road, Morecambe (Tel: 01524-33571)
Liverpool FHC, 4 Mill Bank, Liverpool L13 0BW (Tel: 0151-252-0614)
Manchester FHC, Altrincham Road, Wythenshawe, Manchester M22 4BJ
(Tel: 0161-902-9279)
Preston Temple FHC, Reception Building, Temple Way, Chorley
(Tel: 01257-226145)
Rawtenstall FHC, Haslingden Road, Rawtenstall, Rossendale BB4 0QX
(Tel: 01706-213460)

LEICESTERSHIRE
Leicester FHC, Wakerley Road, Leicester LE5 4WD (Tel: 01162-737334)

LINCOLNSHIRE
Grimsby FHC, Linwood Avenue, Waltham Road, Scartho, Grimsby
  DN33 2PA (Tel: 01472-828876)
Lincoln FHC, LDS Chapel, Skellingthorpe Road, Lincoln LN6 0PB
  (Tel: 01522-680117)

LONDON, GREATER
Hyde Park FHC, 64–68 Exhibition Road, South Kensington, London
  SW7 2PA (Tel: 020-7589-8561)
Wandsworth FHC, 149 Nightingale Lane, Balham, London SW12
  (Tel: 020-8673-6741)

MIDDLESEX
Staines FHC, 41 Kingston Road, Staines TW14 0ND (Tel: 01784-462627)

MIDLANDS, WEST
Coventry FHC, Riverside Close, Whitley, Coventry (Tel: 024-7630-3316)
Harborne FHC, 38 Lordswood Road, Harborne, Birmingham B17 9QS
  (Tel: 0121-553-2137)
Sutton Coldfield FHC, 185 Penns Lane, Sutton Coldfield, Birmingham
  B76 1JU (Tel: 0121-386-1690)
Wednesfield FHC, Linthouse Lane, Wednesfield, Wolverhampton
  (Tel: 01902-724097)

NORFOLK
Kings Lynn FHC, Reffley Lane, Kings Lynn PE30 3EQ
  (Tel: 01553-670000)
Norwich FHC, 19 Greenways, Eaton, Norwich NR4 7AX
  (Tel: 01603-452440)
Thetford FHC, Station Road, Thetford (Tel: 01842-755472)

NORTHAMPTONSHIRE
Northampton FHC, 137 Harlestone Road, Northampton
  (Tel: 0160-458-7630)

NOTTINGHAMSHIRE
Mansfield FHC, Southridge Drive, Mansfield NG18 4RT
(Tel: 01623-26729)
Nottingham FHC, Stanhope Square, West Bridgford, Nottingham NG6
8PA (Tel: 0115-914-4255)

SHROPSHIRE
Telford FHC, 72 Glebe Street, Wellington (Tel: 01952-257443)

SOMERSET
Yeovil FHC, Forest Hill, Yeovil (Tel: 01935-426817)

STAFFORDSHIRE
Lichfield FHC, Purcell Avenue, Lichfield (Tel: 01543-414843)
Newcastle under Lyme FHC, The Brampton, Newcastle under Lyme
ST5 0TV (Tel: 01782-630178)

SUFFOLK
Ipswich FHC, 42 Sidegate Lane West, Ipswich IP4 3DB
(Tel: 01473-723182)
Lowestoft FHC, 165 Yarmouth Road, Lowestoft (Tel: 01502-573851)

SUSSEX (EAST AND WEST)
Crawley FHC, Old Horsham Road, Crawley, West Sussex RH11 8PD
(Tel: 01293-561151)
Hastings FHC, 2 Ledsham Avenue, St Leonards-on-Sea, East Sussex
(Tel: 01424-754563)
Worthing FHC, Goring Street, Worthing, West Sussex
(Tel: 01903-765790)

TYNE AND WEAR
Sunderland FHC, Linden Road, Off Queen Alexandra Road,
Sunderland SR2 9BT (Tel: 0191-528-5787)

WILTSHIRE
Trowbridge FHC, Brook Road, Trowbridge (Tel: 01225-777097)

WORCESTERSHIRE
Redditch FHC, 321 Evesham Road, Crabbs Cross, Redditch B97 5JA
(Tel: 01527-550657)

YORKSHIRE
Huddersfield FHC, 12 Halifax Street, Dewsbury (Tel: 01484-454573)
Hull FHC, 725 Holderness Road, Hull HU4 7RT (Tel: 01482-701439)
Leeds FHC, Vesper Road, Leeds LS5 3QT (Tel: 0113-258-5297)
Pontefract FHC, Park Villas Drive, Pontefract (Tel: 01977-600308)
Scarborough FHC, Stepney Drive/Whitby Road, Scarborough
   (Tel: 01723-501026)
Sheffield FHC, Wheel Lane, Grenoside, Sheffield S30 3RL
   (Tel: 0114-245-3124)
York FHC, West Bank, Acomb, York (Tel: 01904-786784)

WALES
Cardiff FHC, Heol y Deri, Rhiwbina, Cardiff, South Glamorgan
   CF4 6UH (Tel: 029-2062-5342)
Gaerwen FHC, Holyhead Road, Gaerwen, Anglesey (Tel: 01248-421894)
Merthyr Tydfil FHC, Nanty Gwenith Street, George Town, Merthyr
   Tydfil, Mid Glamorgan CF48 1NR (Tel: 01685-722455)
Newcastle Emlyn FHC, Cardigan Road, Newcastle Emlyn
   (Tel: 01269-831170)
Rhyl FHC, Rhuddlan Road, Rhyl, Clwyd (Tel: 01745-331172)
Swansea FHC, LDS Chapel, Cockett Road, Swansea, West Glamorgan
   (Tel: 01792-585792)

SCOTLAND
Aberdeen FHC, North Anderson Drive, Aberdeen, Grampian AB2 6DD
   (Tel: 01224-692206)
Ayr FHC, Orchard Avenue/Mossgiel Road, Ayr (Tel: 01292-610632)
Dumfries FHC, 36 Edinburgh Road, Albanybank, Dumfries
   (Tel: 01387-254865)
Dundee FHC, Bingham Terrace, Dundee, Tayside DD4 7HH
   (Tel: 01382-451247)
Edinburgh FHC, 30a Colinton Road, Edinburgh EH4 3SN
   (Tel: 0131-337-3049)
Elgin FHC, Pansport Road, Elgin, Morayshire (Tel: 01343-546429)
Glasgow FHC, 35 Julian Avenue, Glasgow, Strathclyde G12 0RB
   (Tel: 0141-357-1024)

Inverness FHC, 13 Ness Walk, Inverness, Highlands IV3 5SQ
(Tel: 01463-231220)
Kirkcaldy FHC, Winifred Crescent/Forth Park, Kirkcaldy, Fife
(Tel: 01592-640041)
Lerwick FHC, South Road, Lerwick, Zer Orq, Shetland Islands
(Tel: 01595-695732)
Paisley FHC, Glenburn Road, Paisley, Renfrewshire
(Tel: 0141-884-2780)

NORTHERN IRELAND

Belfast FHC, 403 Holywood Road, Belfast, Co Down BT4 2GU
(Tel: 028-9076-8250)
Coleraine FHC, 8 Sandelfield, Coleraine, Co Londonderry
(Tel: 028-7032-1214)
Londonderry FHC, Racecourse Road, Belmont Estate, Londonderry

REPUBLIC OF IRELAND

Cork FHC, Scarsfield Road, Wilton, Cork (Tel: 00-3531-341737)
Dublin FHC, Ireland Dublin Mission, The Willows, Finglas Road,
Dublin 11 (Tel: 00-3531-8305803)
Limerick FHC, Doraddoyle Road, Limerick (Tel: 00-01595-695732)

FURTHER USEFUL CIVIL REGISTRATION PUBLICATIONS

District Register Offices in England and Wales, East Yorks Family
History Society.
The Parishes, Registers and Registrars of Scotland, Scottish Association
of Family History Societies.
Catherine Blumsom, *Civil Registration of Births, Deaths and Marriages
in Ireland. A Practical Approach,* Ulster Historical Foundation.
Includes a list of Superintendent Registrar's Offices, with telephone
numbers, in the Republic of Ireland.
Kathleen B Cory, *Tracing Your Scottish Ancestry,* Polygon, Edinburgh.

Schedule of Fees and Costs

The published prices are correct at time of publication. The Federation of Family History Societies cannot be held liable for any changes in the fees and costs listed below when buying copy certificates. All figures may be subject to change without prior warning.

In addition to the above certificate costs the following admission fees were also operative for visitors:

ENGLAND AND WALES (Family Records Centre, London)

None; Free admission to the BDM indexes.

General Search in indexes held in local register offices £18.00 per day (NB These are local indexes of births and deaths, and many – though not always all – local marriages. They are not national indexes).

SCOTLAND (New Register House, Edinburgh)

Admission pass per person: Part Day £10, Full Day £17 (£13 discounted APEX place booked from 6 weeks in advance), One week £65, Four Weeks £220, One Quarter £500, One Year £1500. Admission includes access to computerised indexes AND the actual register entries, plus reduced charge of £8.00 per certificate or £2.50 per uncertified photocopy of register entries ordered during visits by valid pass-holders. General Search in local register offices' indexes £10.00 per hour.

NORTHERN IRELAND (Oxford House, Belfast)

Admission by different search fees. Five-year search, or part, for one event only £3.00; Search in BDM indexes for a period not exceeding 6 hours (including 4 free verifications from indexes - additional verifications £1 each) £6.00; Search of BDM records assisted by member of staff (must be pre-booked) £15.00 per hour.

REPUBLIC OF IRELAND (Joyce House, Dublin)

Admission by "Particular Search" for one event over a period not exceeding five years IR£1.50; or by "General Search" for any event in the B and D indexes not exceeding 6 hours, or any event in the M indexes during any successive days not exceeding six - IR£12.00.

ISLE OF MAN (Registries Building, Douglas)

None; Free admission to BDM indexes.

JERSEY (Royal Square, St Helier)

None, but very limited access to records 9-11am daily by appointment.

GUERNSEY (Royal Court House, St Peter Port)

£1.00 per person from 2.00pm to 4.00pm only on normal weekdays when there is public access to the Strong Room and details can be copied from the records.

Current costs of certificates and/or search fees can be obtained by telephoning the main national offices or from their websites.

COUNTRY	Visit in person with full Reference	By post with full reference (no request for search in indexes)	By post without reference (with search)	Priority Search (Certificate supplied very quickly)	Ordered via Internet	At Local Register Offices (in person or by post)
England And Wales	£6.50	£8.00	£11.00 with 3-year search	£24.00 with reference £27.00 without	N/A	£6.50
Scotland	£11.00	£13.00	£13.00	Cert + £10.00	£16.00	£13.00
Northern Ireland	£4.00	£4.00	£7.00	Cert + £10.00	N/A	£7.00
Republic of Ireland	IR£5.50	IR£5.50, or uncertified photocopy IR£1.50	IR£5.50, or uncertified photocopy IR£3.00	N/A	N/A	IR£5.50 in person IR£5.80 by post
Isle of Man	£5.60	£5.60	£5.60 + £2.75 per year searched	N/A	N/A	N/A
Jersey	£7.00	£7.00 plus £1.00 airmail, or 50p UK post	£7.00 + £5.00 per 5-year search B or D indexes, or + £10.00 per 5-year search M indexes	N/A	N/A	N/A
Guernsey	£5.00	£5.00	£5.00	N/A	N/A	N/A

NOTES

NOTES

NOTES

NOTES

NOTES